Twayne's United States Authors Series

EDITOR OF THIS VOLUME

Warren French

Indiana University

William Goldman

TUSAS 326

WILLIAM GOLDMAN

By RICHARD ANDERSEN
Boston University

TWAYNE PUBLISHERS
A DIVISION OF G. K. HALL & CO., BOSTON

Printed on permanent / durable acid-free paper and bound
in the United States of America

First Printing

Frontispiece photo of William Goldman
by Ilene Jones

Library of Congress Cataloging in Publication Data

Andersen, Richard, 1946–
William Goldman.

(Twayne's United States authors series ; TUSAS 326)
Bibliography: p.
Includes index.
1. Goldman, William, 1931–
—Criticism and interpretation.
PS3557.0384Z53   813'.5'4   78–13260
ISBN 0–8057–7259–6

For: JESS

Contents

About the Author

Richard Andersen is a professor of Humanities at Boston University. He holds degrees from Loyola University of Los Angeles, Richmond College of the City University of New York, and New York University. His other works include *The Straight Cut Ditch*, a novel in the *Bildungsroman* tradition, and *Ants in a Sponge*, a fictional history of the Muckaluck Indian war.

Preface

Before the paperback publication of *Boys and Girls Together* in 1965, William Goldman was a virtually unknown and often misunderstood writer. Reviewers of his first novel, *The Temple of Gold* (1957), compared him to Ernest Hemingway and F. Scott Fitzgerald; later ones associated him with John Knowles, S. J. Wilson, and J. D. Salinger. Goldman's second book, *Your Turn to Curtsy, My Turn to Bow* (1958), was not mentioned in a review until 1966, and his partially humorous treatment of military life in *Soldier in the Rain* (1960) won him comparisons not with Joseph Heller, as is the case today, but rather with television's Sergeant Bilko. With subsequent novels came critical associations with Saul Bellow, J. R. Tolkien, Franz Kafka, Robert Louis Stevenson, and Jonathan Swift. As flattering as these associations may be, however, they are so various that they fail to be accurate. Having been compared to Hemingway, Fitzgerald, Knowles, Wilson, Salinger, Heller, Bellow, Tolkien, Kafka, Stevenson, Swift, and Sergeant Bilko, it is a wonder that Goldman has a reputation as a writer in his own right.

In spite of the complimentary identifications, ten novels, five screenplays, two stage-plays, a children's story, a book-length criticism of the contemporary theater, Motion Picture Academy Awards for the Best Original Screenplay of 1969 and the Best Screenplay Adaptation from Another Medium of 1976, creative writing appointments at Princeton and New York universities, more film adaptations from his novels than any of the above-mentioned authors, the attention of critics such as Edward Albee and John Simon, and a worldwide readership, Goldman's works have been ignored by literary scholars.

The first purpose of this book, then, is to give to Goldman the attention his works not only merit but need if they are to survive the inaccurate praise of newspapermen and magazine critics. The book's second purpose is to analyze in detail the texts of Goldman's works as they develop his theme of young men and women whose untried ideals are challenged and, in most cases, altered by their individual circumstances. This is the most appropriate theme for a first critical study on Goldman for several reasons. It is the·central theme of his early novels and the problem that he undertakes to solve in his later works. It has never been adequately discussed by critics, who have chosen to comment upon each of Goldman's works as individual pieces rather than as an oeuvre in which a single theme is developed.

Because it is the main concern of all his works, Goldman's theme of young men and women trying to incorporate their ideals with an uncompromising reality serves as the perfect springboard from which to discuss the author's view of such significant issues as the transforming power of the imagination, the inherent destructiveness of idealistic trends of thought, the result of unrealistic expectations, guilt and the necessity of action to overcome it, the spiritual condition of middle-class Jewish-Americans, mankind's need to flee the meaningless experiences of everyday life, and the results of such escapes. These secondary issues are as important as Goldman's central theme because of the representation he gives them and the help they afford in establishing Goldman's place in the context of escapist literature, that is, in the tradition of writers whose concerns center on people trying to escape from realities with which they are unprepared to cope.

In order to facilitate a clear understanding of the development of Goldman's treatment of young people who struggle to cope with reality, his novels are treated chronologically. If there seems to be some sort of mechanical pattern developing in this chronology as the book evolves, the development is probably organic rather than managed, as escape is the common denominator of all Goldman's works. Nevertheless, the peculiarities of the times in which Goldman has written have helped shape and mold the characteristics of each novel. Hence, the nature of Raymond Trevitt's escape in *The Temple of Gold* (1957) is quite different from and, in fact, sharply contrasts with Corky Wither's escape in *Magic* (1976).

Each chapter of the book, then, discusses a particular phase of Goldman's developing theme along with the secondary but equally important issues pertinent to the novels discussed in that chapter. The presentation of the issues is enriched by excerpts from the author's personal interview with Goldman that took place in February of 1976. That part of the interview not referred to in the chapters pertaining to Goldman's novels provides this book's first chapter, in which Goldman discusses his attitudes toward his works and his profession in general. In addition, references are made throughout the book to Goldman's screenplays, screenplay adaptations, stage-plays, children's story, unpublished short stories, and critical efforts. Through these works and his novels, some of which are out of print as hardbacks and must be referred to through the paperback editions, Goldman creates not only a picture of the important personal but universal issues confronting twentieth-century Americans, but also a portrait of the men and women who are facing these issues and responding to them.

RICHARD ANDERSEN

Boston University

Acknowledgments

I wish to extend a special note of gratitude to Professor J. B. Bessinger, Jr., without whose constant encouragement, patient criticism, and cheerful devotion neither this book nor what I am today would have been possible.

I also would like to acknowledge my appreciation to Jackie Andersen and Robert Hendersen, who first introduced me to William Goldman's novels; to William Goldman, who, in conversations in his home and office in New York, supplied me with biographical data and valuable information concerning his writings; to Yvonne Martinez, who was the manuscript's first proofreader and a genuine inspiration; to Janet Deegan, who supported me through and eagerly proofread the book's final draft; to Profesors Warren French and John Kuehl, who provided generous and intelligent editorial assistance; and to Professor James W. Tuttleton, who read the manuscript, made many helpful suggestions en route, and commissioned the Fales Special Collections Library in New York to establish a permanent collection of William Goldman's works and memorabilia.

Others who gave of their time and energies are: Bobby Forrest, Stewart Tabakin, Sigfried Heiles, and Bruce Forer.

Chronology

1931 Born August 12, Chicago, Illinois.

1952 Graduated from Oberlin College with a Bachelor of Arts degree in English.

1952– Served in the United States Armed Forces. Honorably dis-
1954 charged with the rank of corporal.

1954– Received Master of Arts degree in Theatre from Columbia
1956 University and completed the course requirements for a Doctor of Philosophy degree in literature.

1957 *The Temple of Gold.*

1958– *Your Turn to Curtsy, My Turn to Bow;* "Something Blue" in
1959 *Rogue* magazine; "Till the Right Girls Come Along" in *Transatlantic Review;* also two unpublished short stories: "Now I am Six" and "The Simple Pleasures of the Rich."

1960 *Soldier in the Rain.*

1961 Married to Ilene Jones; *Blood, Sweat, and Stanley Poole,* coauthored with James Goldman, produced on Broadway.

1962 *Family Affair,* coauthored with John Kander and James Goldman, produced on Broadway; daughter, Jennifer Rebecca, born.

1964 *Boys and Girls Together; No Way to Treat a Lady* (under the pseudonym Harry Longbaugh).

1965 Daughter, Susanna, born.

1965– Taught creative writing at Princeton University.
1966

1966 *Harper,* screenplay adaptation of Ross MacDonald's novel, *The Moving Target.*

1967 *The Thing of It Is . . . . The Chill,* unproduced sequel to *Harper,* adapted from Ross MacDonald's novel of the same title.

1968 *In The Spring The War Ended,* unproduced screenplay, adapted from Steven Linakis's novel of the same title.

1969 *The Season: A Candid Look at Broadway; Butch Cassidy and the Sundance Kid,* an original screenplay; "The Good-Bye

Look," a review of Ross MacDonald's novel, *New York Times Book Review*.

1970 *The Thing of It Is . . .,* unproduced screenplay adaptation from the novel of the same title; *Butch Cassidy and the Sundance Kid* voted the Best Original Screenplay of 1969 by the Academy of Motion Picture Arts and Sciences.

1971 *Father's Day.*

1972 *The Hot Rock,* screenplay adaptation from Donald Westlake's novel of the same title.

1973 *The Princess Bride.*

1974 *The Princess Bride,* unproduced screenplay adaptation from the novel; *Wigger; The Stepford Wives,* screenplay adaptation from Ira Levin's novel of the same title; *Marathon Man; Mr. Horn,* an unproduced original screenplay, sold in 1978 to United Artists as a television miniseries.

1975 *The Great Waldo Pepper,* an original screenplay.

1976 *All the President's Men,* screenplay adaptation from Bob Woodward and Carl Bernstein's book of the same title; *Marathon Man,* screenplay adaptation from the novel of the same title; *Magic.*

1977 *All the President's Men* voted the Best Screenplay Adapted from Another Medium in 1976 by the Academy of Motion Picture Arts and Sciences; *A Bridge Too Far,* screenplay adaptation of Cornelius Ryan's book of the same title.

1978 *Magic,* screenplay adaptation from the novel of the same title.

CHAPTER 1

Goldman on Goldman

I   On Becoming a Writer

IN 1956, William Goldman was a desperate man. He had always wanted to be a writer, yet he had never written anything that was much longer than two pages. He had taken a creative writing course at Oberlin College and another at Northwestern University, but had received the lowest grade in each class. He had been the story editor of Oberlin's literary magazine, but had failed to get any of his short stories printed in it. By 1956, Goldman was twenty-four years old. "I had been in the army for two years, and I had taken two years to get my master's. I had the hours for a doctorate, but I'm not good at languages, and I didn't want to spend a year of my life learning three of them."

Goldman's family, which is comprised mostly of businessmen from the Middle West, felt that their would-be writer would probably go into advertising. The summer after he received his Master of Arts in Theatre from Columbia University, however, Goldman wrote his first novel. "*The Temple of Gold* was an act of desperation. That was it! I couldn't get a story accepted. If *The Temple of Gold* hadn't been accepted, I would have gone on to be a copywriter in Chicago. Fortunately, they were looking for first novelists at that time, and my book fit in, so it was taken.

"I don't know where I got the idea to become a writer. I always wanted to be a writer. My brother, who is four and one half years older than I am, wanted to be a writer. Maybe I got the idea from him. I don't know. I thought being a writer would be neat, but nobody told me what being a writer was like. I don't like the act of writing. I don't enjoy writing. I don't think I'm a good writer. I never reread what I write until the time comes when I have a talk with somebody crucial, usually an editor if it's a book or a director if it's a movie. I'll read it then, once, that's all.

15

"Once *The Temple of Gold* was taken, I went for a year not doing anything and basically feeling like a bum. I flagellated myself, and wrote *Your Turn to Curtsy, My Turn to Bow* in seven days. The only book I've ever written which I am really proud of is *The Princess Bride*. Second to that is my children's book, *Wigger*, which I wrote immediately after *The Princess Bride*, when I was still hanging around in fantasy storytelling. Now, that doesn't mean that they're good, but those are the only books that I was really happy writing.

"There are reasons why I've been dissatisfied with my books. I was, at one time, a good reader, and I read my Dostoevsky, and my Tolstoy, and my Dickens, and my Balzac, and I am obsessed with the way reality looks like toothpaste when I write it. It's in my head that 'Oh, boy, I'm going to write a really great scene,' and I get to my office, and I'm there, and I write, and it comes out very bland, and it's not what I meant at all. I envy certain writers, who, when they get in trouble, can figure out what their trouble is. I can't do that. I don't mean to sound dramatic, but it's one of the reasons why I don't like my writing very much. I remember there was a quote from James Jones. It was just after he got all that heat for *From Here to Eternity*, and he said, 'I can look at any page of that book and know it was exactly that way I meant it to be,' and I thought, in my own case, I can tell there is usually a scene in each book that I can look at without humiliation, and say, 'Gee, that's as good as I can do.'

"Today, I'm always very negative whenever I get letters that say, 'I want to be a writer. What do I do?' I say, 'Don't do it. Don't do it. It's a terrible life. It's a life of frustration. You'll end up drinking too much. There's little financial renumeration and little recognition.' I tend to do that because if anything I can say will make anybody stop from being a writer, they wouldn't be a writer anyway. And nobody ever told me when I was growing up that it was a shitty life, and so I make sure, if I can, that if anybody asks me to be as blunt as I can possibly be as to what the realities of trying to survive as a creative writer in this country are at this time, I tell them because nobody told me."

II   *On Being a Writer*

"I have very strange feelings about being a writer. For example, today I was sent a novel by a well-known writer who wants a quotation from me about his new book. Now, what's difficult is, he gave a quotation to a publisher once about a novel of mine. Now, I've never done that. In my whole life, I've never given a quotation. I've had dear friends, who have said, 'Would you read my book and if you like it, would you give me a quote?' And I have never given a quotation to anybody because I have never wanted to get caught up in one of those things where I praise your book and you praise my book. I always thought being a writer meant having a certain amount of integrity, and I don't give quotations at this point. I don't think I'm supposed to be a whore. I just try to stay in my pit and write my books. I don't write my books to sell. In point of fact, they don't sell, except in paperback. They've all been critically not well received by the intellectual centers.

"Writing is basically antisocial. You go into a room. That's an antisocial act, and you stay there. Some people never come out, but most of us do, occasionally, and I'm a husband and a father and trying to live a 'normal' life in New York. What's difficult for me now about writing is not communing with my deep philosophical thoughts, because I don't do that, but just getting through the day in the silence. I can't take the silence anymore, so I have records going.

"Recently, I was asked by the *London Telegraph* to do an interview on *The Bridge Too Far*. Now, a reporter is basically a social animal. Even though he's a writer, he doesn't write out of his own head. He writes out of interviews. Anyway, this reporter met me in my office, and there was music playing because I always write now with music of some kind. I said to him, 'Do you mind it?' And he said, 'Why is it on?' And I said, 'Because I always have some kind of sound.' And he said, 'Why?' And I said, 'Because I can't take the silence anymore. I've been writing for so long; I'm about to enter my third decade of it. And the reality of writing is that nobody gives a shit what you do if you're a writer because, until there's something finished, you go into a hole by yourself, and there's silence all day long. I can't stand the silence anymore, so I have sound.'

"The records had stopped by this point, and I said, 'The silence is really hard to take. Now what I would like you to do is be quiet for a couple of seconds.' And he said, 'Well it must be very diffi . . .' And I said, 'No, no, no. Be quiet. Don't talk.' And he said, 'Well, I can see . . .' And I said, 'No, you're still talking. You must be quiet. You must listen to the silence.' And he wouldn't. And I couldn't make him shut up for five seconds. And then, the next day, when he called me about taking a picture, he said, 'What I'm writing about is the silence.' I knew that the silence had hit something in him, and I knew that he would never write, which may make him a better or worse person. There's no judgment on that. It's just that that's what I find hard. Doing it everyday is hard."

III   *On Teaching Others to Write*

"When I taught at Princeton University, I had twelve students and four of them had talent. In the opening class, I read *The Little Engine That Could* to them. It was a class in narrative writing, and, as you know, that's about as clean an example of narrative writing as there is. There are only about six adjectives. 'The poor little train,' or whatever it is, 'said, "I think I can. I think I can."' It's almost pure narrative, and it's a super story on that level. It's very clear. It tells you right at the top who are the good guys and who are the bad guys. Whatever Dostoevsky or Cervantes did is all in that nutty little story.

"The students, I think, hated being read the story because they felt I was demeaning their skills. It was probably something they would have appreciated more if they knew I was on their side, which in point of fact I was, but they had no way of knowing that then because they were Princeton students and fairly hostile. At any rate, after that I read them nothing. I would only read their stories out loud without saying whose stories they were, and that's a fascinating experience. No student could get too vicious because it might be him the next week, and yet he couldn't be too nice either because everybody would know he was bullshitting. When the class went well, there was a certain amount of give and take, and it was all very pleasant. The problem with it was it took so much time and it was debilitating as far as my writing was concerned. I did not write that year. I gave it all to teaching.

"Once I finished the opening class and explained what I thought they should try and deal with at the age of twenty-one, which was trying to handle narrative, the inevitable beginning of their stories, which I would harass them about, would be: 'He rolled up on his elbow and looked at her.' It was always sort of ludicrous. There were no girls there yet, and the Princeton boys would all write the same wish fulfillment. What they'd really do is get drunk, but they would maintain the other image for themselves when they wrote.

"It's very difficult to teach someone to write creatively. I was, at that point in my life, a professional writer. I had just written my first screenplay, called *Harper*, which was eventually made into a movie

with Paul Newman, and I had three or four novels published. I was
thirty-something years old, and it's very damaging to say to a kid
who's written a story his way, 'You've told the story wrong. Let me
show you how it should be done.' Then you write it for him. All you
could do, because all you had was your own ear and eye, was make the
student verbalize as much as possible what he was trying to do and
then try and give him the support he needed.

IV   *On the Reasons for Being a Writer*

"The theory that I guess I believe in, which I don't know if it's
original or not, is that basically writers are like teeter-totters. We're
trying to make it balance. We had miserable childhoods, whether we
were rich or poor, and we're trying to make the teeter-totter balance.
We were ignored or spurned or whatever when we were between the
ages of zero and five or six, and our writing is an act of revenge. I'm
getting the teeter-totter back so that I'm looking good and you're
looking bad. Vengeance is a very strong-sounding word. Retaliation
might be better, but I don't think so. Writing is an act of revenge.

"I have very few original thoughts, but I'll give you one. This is said
pontifically: One of the troubles with novels, I think, is that they're all
written by novelists, by which I mean that there's not a lot of
difference between me and the worst writer you can think of,
whoever he may be, in terms of what it is that makes us go to our pits
and work each day. I wish someday the Ford Foundation would
randomly select twenty-five people, whether they be morons or
housewives or intellectuals or anything, and say, 'We'll give you ten
thousand dollars, stop your jobs, and turn in two hundred pages of
double-spaced, typed, about anything you want. No one will know
who wrote what because it will all be coded. You can put down
whatever you want to.' For all we know, there will be books about
flowers, or maybe there'll be books about violent sex, or maybe
there'll be books about summer. I'd love to know what a cabdriver has
to say, but he can't write it. I'm serious because basically what we end
up with now is a neurosis of people like me.

"I suppose the reason I've done so much movie writing over the
last 'X' years has been because it's nice to be wanted. If I do a book
every two years, that's a lot, and I have to have something to do in that
space of time, which means the movies happen to fit because I have a
certain skill for it, and there has been affection for me there. I have a

theory about artists. I think they gravitate toward affection and softness and gentleness and receptivity, and I wrote a number of short stories once, and one of them was really good. It was called 'The Simple Pleasures of the Rich.' Anyway, the intense rejection from everybody of what was the best I could do made me stop writing short stories. My agent at that time happened to also like the story and set off on a campaign to get the thing published. I think she eventually ended up with something like sixty or seventy-five rejection slips for the one story, so I went on to doing movies between novels. Screenplays haven't been like the short stories. I haven't been beating my head against the wall trying to get a screenplay accepted. It's nice to be wanted.

"Two and a half years ago, I happened to succumb to a rare strain of pneumonia. The head neurologist at New York Hospital found that the last time it had ever been written about was in 1937. I was hospitalized, and was phenomenally weak for months afterwards. One of the side effects of the pneumonia, which is how they were able to diagnose it, is a loss of vision in my right eye. When I got out of the hospital, and I was forty-two, I was suddenly obsessed with the fact that I had a lovely wife and two lovely daughters, and I was mortal. Over the last two years, since I got my strength back, I've written a sickening amount of material. I've written a novel, *Marathon Man*, and that means the rewriting of the novel and the galley proofs and the page proofs. I've just written a new novel called *Magic*. I wrote a children's book called *Wigger*. I wrote the screenplay and the rewriting and the rewriting and the rewriting of *All the President's Men*. I wrote the original screenplay and two rewrites of a western called *Mr. Horn*. I wrote the screenplay and three entire rewrites of the screenplay of *Marathon Man*. I wrote the screenplay and one rewrite of *The Princess Bride*, which is my one novel I really care about.

"Now, there's a wonderful phrase, I think, called 'fuck-you money.' I want my 'fuck-you money' so I don't have to work anymore except on things I care to work on. The reason I have this mustache is because I lost the vision in my right eye when I got sick. After being in bed for a month, I had a beard. One day, when I was feeling some strength, I was shaving, and the kids and my wife were in the bedroom. Each time I would shave off a section of my beard, I would go into the bedroom and say, 'Da-Dah!' The last thing that I took off was this gunfighter's mustache. The reason it's as long as it is, is because I cannot see the right half of my face. The only way I can make the mustache come out even is to feel along my chinbone. It's my death mustache. It makes me very much aware of the fact that I was very sick, and I could be very sick again. The reason I have worked with this ferocity is partially neurotic, to avoid facing reality, and partially because I am, at this point in the movie business, as hot as I'm ever going to be, and I want to get out before they get me out."

V *Writing for the Movies*

"As a general rule, screenwriting is not something about which I care a great deal. It's a craft. At first it's interesting. Each time it brings up certain problems that have to be solved. For example, on *The Bridge Too Far*, the problem on the first draft was to write a script that a) made sense—because the book is six hundred pages long and very complicated, and b) had a sufficient number of star parts. Obviously I was successful in my attempt at getting the cast.

"But each movie is different and each first draft has a different problem. You may have to succor a director; you may have to pacify a star; you may have to do whatever it is. After the first draft, however, you're dealing with technical things because movies are basically technical and group endeavors.

"In the movies, one does the best one can, always, and then you have to deal with the other egos that are around, not just your own, which is enormous in my case, clearly, but also the director's, whose is more enormous because he's more highly paid, and the star's, which is the greatest of all because he's the most highly paid.

"When Hollywood found they needed writers, which is when sound came in, they bought silence by overpaying. Do your job when you're supposed to do it, and then be quiet. I don't have a lot of friends in the picture business because I have a lot of ego, and I'll say, 'No, you're wrong. That's a good scene. Leave it.' But the reality is, it's not my problem. For example, on *All the President's Men*, I did an original and a rewrite and then another rewrite, and that was it. I haven't talked to anybody on that film since April of '75 and now it's February of '76. They started shooting in May. I don't know what the movie's like. I worked for a long time on *Papillon*, and then the budget began to skyrocket, while I was working on *The Great Waldo Pepper*, and they needed a second star, so what they did was they brought in several other writers, who compressed all of the secondary roles into one for Dustin Hoffman. There's one line of mine left in the movie. I have no idea what *Marathon Man* is going to be like.

"There's a women's liberation phrase I use, which is called 'shitwork,' which means, specifically, work that is only noticed when it is done badly, i.e., the diapers or anything having to do with around the house. If the house is clean, the husband does not come home and say, 'Gee, what a clean house!' He only comes home and says, 'What is this pigpen that I have to come home to after breaking my ass?' Screenwriting is basically shitwork. It's only noticed if it's bad. And the reality is, enough of that erodes the soul.

"If there is any interest in me now, it's because of the movies. I don't write my novels for the movies, and I don't consider who my audience is. Saul Bellow stopped an interviewer in the *Times* when he said, 'There are two kinds of writers. There are big audience writers and small audience writers. I'm a big audience writer.' He wants to sell best-sellers. People want you to be off in your garret thinking, 'No one will ever read this, but when I'm dead, Van Gogh will be whatever.' But the reality is of course you would like to sell. We all want our books to be read. One of the reasons I would love *The Princess Bride* to be a movie is because I want the book to sell."

VI   *Writers and Reviewers*

"I've only written one review in my life, a one-page article on the front page of the *New York Times Book Review*, which made Ross MacDonald a cult figure. It was a good review, but it was the *Times* that gave MacDonald its 'Good Housekeeping Seal of Approval.' The year before, they had given Kurt Vonnegut the same thing for *Slaughterhouse-Five*. He was already a cult figure, but that review made him okay. I have never had that stamp in New York because the decision has been made that I've been around, and I've been beaten. The one exception to this is *No Way to Treat a Lady*, which was published under the name of Harry Longbaugh. Anthony Boucher reviewed it and gave it a marvelous notice. It stunned me that such an establishment journal as the *New York Times* could say something nice about something I had written.

"*Butch Cassidy* did not get one rave review in New York in the sense that it could be reprinted in its entirety. Outside of New York, however, it got phenomenal reviews, but I was living in New York, and had been for twenty years on Seventy-fifth Street. George Roy Hill lived on Eighty-seventh Street, Robert Redford lived on Eighty-sixth Street, and Paul Newman lived in Connecticut, but he had an apartment on Fifty-fifth Street. I remember walking with Hill

several days after the movie opened, and we were with a publicity
man as we passed the Sutton, which is a theatre on Fifty-seventh
Street, and the PR guy who was with us said, 'Let's stop in.' When we
were introduced to the manager, he practically embraced us. We
asked him why he was so happy, and he told us, 'Oh, it's just wild.
We're doing a fantastic business.' I remember saying, 'Yeah? Is it?'
And he said, 'A Smash!' And I said, 'Maybe it's not a disaster after all.'
But *Butch* is still a great failure in our minds because the initial
reaction of the critics in New York was so negative.

"They had a big screening for *Butch*, for which they hired a theater
in New York, and held a preview of 'One Thousand Opinion Makers,'
as they were called then. The movie died. It was awful, just awful. I
remember sitting in the last row of the theater, and I was pressing,
and I kept saying, 'Why don't they like it?' No one said they liked it,
and I was crushed. I never went to see the movie again until it was
revived about a year ago. I took my kids and my wife, and it was like a
Gilbert and Sullivan because the audience was laughing and reacting
before the lines because they had all seen it. I've only seen it once
with a paying audience, and I'll never again watch a movie with a
bunch of opinion makers. George Abbott, who started me in the
theater, used to say, 'Warm bodies; people who don't pay are not to
be trusted.'

"Critics usually aren't very good; that's why they're critics. They'd
love to get out of being critics—unless of course, like Robert Kirsch of
the *Los Angeles Times*, they're compulsive readers. Because of my
success in the movie world, what will happen is that every future
review on me will accuse me of writing a novel so that I can turn it into
a screenplay. I wouldn't dream of doing that. They're two different
forms. I care about the one, and I don't care that much about the
other. I've been involved with movies over the last couple of years,
but I expect to uninvolve myself. I don't expect to make a new movie
job that isn't something of mine. If I can sell a new novel to the
movies, terrific, because that's why, frankly, the book will sell."

VII   *Future Prospects*

"There was some talk once about turning *Boys and Girls* into a
television novel, but the whole thing aborted. I would assume it's not
such a dead issue anymore because *Rich Man, Poor Man* is doing
well. It's a wonderful notion; the English do it. It doesn't leave you
with this cursed thing of everything having to be fifty-two minutes or

a two-parter. People can let the story run as long as they want to and then chop it up for commercials when they want to. When the English run out of ideas, they say, 'Okay, that's it.' *All in the Family* will just keep going and going as long as people keep watching. They'll make up permutations and combinations. Shaw's adaptation will open up the possibilities of television not being quite so rancid.

"I think they like me in the movie business because the movies I've written have gotten made. *Marathon Man* may stink, but the word now is 'Wow.' It's the big picture for Paramount for this year, and they're all very high on it, and no one has seen it yet. The point is that all of that is going to go through people's heads when they read my new novel, and they're going to say, 'He's hot. Maybe we can line him.' This is okay with me because I want my novel to be read, but it has nothing to do with quality. It has to do with the fact that they might have a shot at getting a movie made, and there aren't that many movies being made anymore. I'm serious about my novels, but, in a sense, I'm like Conan Doyle. I've gotten successful on something I don't care that much about. He thought of himself as a serious writer, but what anybody ever cared about in terms of popularity was Sherlock Holmes.

"I know now what my next novel is going to be. I've never had that experience before. I've been able to say when I finish one book, I know what the sequel will be, but never another novel. I'm going to write my Hollywood novel. I won't write it from anywhere between six months to a year and a half from now, but I'll say one of my main characters is an actor, and in order for my plot to work, he has to be at a stage in his career where he is on the brink of becoming famous. At the same time, in order for the plot to work, he has to be offered an enormous amount of money to do something. The conflict is, why would you offer an enormous amount of money to somebody who is not famous?

"I am an extremely established screenwriter now, and it's not something I care about. It's maddening in a strange sense because the reality is that it impinges on my career as a novelist, and it will continue to do so until I give it up. The review of my next novel will say that I wrote the book to be made into a movie, and I will be cursed with that kind of review from now on. It will be that way until, I suppose, I cut my umbilical cord by writing my nonfiction book about Hollywood and become persona non grata in Southern California. The only subject besides Hollywood that I'm interested in is sports. That's interesting enough to spend two years on."

VIII *Influences*

"I don't know who my influences are. I know that the book that was crucial to me when I was growing up was Phillip Wiley's *Finnley Wren*, which I read when I was thirteen or fourteen. Then, when I was seventeen, I was given Irwin Shaw's *Mixed Company*, and that was a crucial gift. I guess Shaw, for me, along with Fitzgerald and Updike, are the three most graceful writers we've produced in this country. I couldn't believe how good *Mixed Company* was. It had a tremendous effect on me. It reemphasized the notion that I was going to be a writer. No one ever took that very seriously, and I had to be perfectly frank—I'd shown no signs of any talent.

"I suppose the major influences were Winnie the Pooh, the fact that I love sports, the fact that I love heroes. It's hard to say. *The Temple of Gold* was influenced by J. D. Salinger in the sense that it's written in a very close first person, and *Catcher* was written in a very close first person. It's a very easy thing for writers to begin with because they don't have to worry about what's going on in the other room because they can't see it. I'm aware in my work that there's a progression from *The Temple of Gold*, in a very close first person, to *Your Turn to Curtsy, My Turn to Bow*, which is both first and third person. *Soldier in the Rain* is third person. *Your Turn to Curtsy, My Turn to Bow* is a transition in terms of style. I wasn't totally able to leave first person, and there are time shifts.

"I view myself as a storyteller. Because I'm educated and have read all the books that I'm supposed to have read, I hope that something attaches itself to my story like a snowball on a good packing day when you roll a snowball and it gets bigger. I hope that there are things that attach themselves to the central story that have echoes or ramifications or whatever. I'm not one of those writers that puts in literary allusions, but I have no doubt that they're there because I've read a great deal. What I'm doing consciously, if you ask me, in general the answer would be: 'Well, I had to get the characters to that bar so they could see the drunk.' That'll be why. I want to get from Point A to the point of where my story will end.

"My great fear as a writer is that you'll stop reading me. I tend to be too zippy. I'll have too many paragraphs. The most terrible thing to me is to be told, 'I can't finish it because I know that I'm not one of those compulsive-about-finishing-a-novel readers. If I'm bored, forget it.' The most terrible thing you can do to a writer is to say, 'He bores me.'"

CHAPTER 2

Confronting Reality:
The Temple of Gold

I never would have continued as a writer if *The Temple of Gold* had not been taken by the first publisher I sent it to. I'm not that masochistic. There was no way I was going to write anymore. I didn't know that then, but I know it now. There was no encouragement; no one ever said I had any talent. I had never written anything much over two pages long. I had done badly in school in terms of writing. I did not want to be a failure, but I did not have the courage to write a second book if the first had not been accepted" (WG).

In many ways, *The Temple of Gold* reflects the situation of its young author. Both Goldman and the protagonist, Raymond Trevitt, want to make something of their lives, but are afraid of failing to attain the goals they have set for themselves. Because Goldman lacked confidence in his narrative abilities, he placed his interesting characters, dialogue, and themes into a plot structure that prevented him from establishing his maturity as a writer with his first novel. Raymond Trevitt, on the other hand, wants to be an adult, but he does not know what it means to be one. Afraid of failing to mature, he often retreats from situations that might initiate him into adulthood. *The Temple of Gold*, then, is a novel that attempted to initiate William Goldman into the vocation of writing and Raymond Trevitt into adulthood.

As in most novels of initiation, Raymond Trevitt is innocent but not completely naive. He is not corrupted by evil, but he can recognize it in others. On the other hand, he fails to recognize how dangerous his ignorance of adult realities is to others. Raymond's first reaction is to retreat from realities that might initiate him into adulthood, but he eventually decides to confront him. Because he cannot surrender the cherished ideals of his youth, however, Raymond fails to become an adult. Consequently, *The Temple of Gold* leaves its young protagonist having reached but not crossed the borderline of maturity.

Goldman's first novel is in the *Bildungsroman* tradition, yet its treatment of the central conflict, between innocence and experience, is not traditional. Raymond Trevitt is neither a symbol of purity and true insight nor an embodiment of any of the simplicities usually identified with innocence in America. On the contrary, his ignorance of adult sensibilities often causes pain to himself and to those with whom he comes in contact. Because he is innocent, however, Raymond fails to make the proper connection between his naiveté and the pain it inflicts. Searching for a place in the adult world that will accept him and protect his childhood innocence at the same time, Raymond discovers failure, old age, and death—that of his father and two close friends. Unable to internalize these immitigable realities, Raymond never realizes an adult appreciation of the value of life and continues to be a threat to the well-being of others.

Although Raymond is dangerous, he also embodies that one cohesive principle, love, that most lends itself to the preservation of life. That Raymond can be both a destroyer and a preserver of life may be a characteristic of his adolescent nature, but the contradiction should not be misinterpreted as the felt contradictions that history has imposed on the American tradition of innocence. Raymond is an adolescent, not a representative man. His experience and his perspectives are certainly broad enough for him to offer a significant response to the world he inhabits, but his lack of articulate critical self-consciousness prevents him from offering a serious comment on the adult world at large.

Raymond's initiation into adult values, as well as his awakening to the dangers of his innocence, begins in childhood. Had Raymond known, for example, that it was possible to overfeed guppies, his love for his father's fish and his good intention to take care of them would not have resulted in their death and his being severely beaten. Raymond's innocence, Goldman seems to be saying, is basically a dangerous ignorance. Furthermore, it is the root cause of the disproportion that exists between his good intention (feeding the guppies) and its practical application (death and punishment). This disproportion, which allows Raymond to be innocent of murder but guilty of the fish's deaths, creates the dilemma which he searches for a way to resolve throughout *The Temple of Gold*. Raymond's quest is to find a situation in life where his idealistic intentions are not disproportionate to the everyday reality in which they are enacted. Such a position, however, is philosophically untenable. Its conclusion negates its premise. Raymond cannot participate in the world and protect his innocent ideals at the same time.

The phenomenon of disproportion is one of the external problems of life and of all great literature, and Goldman recognizes that his perception of it may have been shaped by other writers. Among those whom he has cited as possible influences are Balzac, Dickens, Dostoevsky, and Tolstoy. Each of these writers concerns himself, among other things, with how men and women may achieve victory over the disproportion that exists between intention and reality. In *The Temple of Gold*, Goldman too was concerned with this question. However, only twenty-four years old, he understandably could not approach the narrative and symbolic level of the writers who had influenced him. Raymond's guppies are a far cry from the masters mentioned above, but they are symbols drawn from life and represent the apprentice writer's attempt to deal with important issues.

Through Zock, a boy of Raymond's age but superior to him in intelligence and experience, Goldman's hero finds the understanding that his parents fail to provide. The boys' relationship is the first of many male relationships in Goldman's writing. In each of these latently homosexual encounters, at least one of the males is searching for someone who will protect his innocence. Says Goldman, "What I would like to think is not that I'm a closet queen, but that it has to do with searching for someone of your own sex who will protect you. I am aware of the fact that what I tend to write best are male-to-male relationships, but the only time I've dealt remotely specifically with homosexuality was in *Boys and Girls Together*, and that's very gingerly treated. What I tend to think is that what I'm doing is not so much homosexuality as it is a search for a defender."

When Raymond and Zock hitchhike to Chicago, they are picked up by a homosexual who is ready to take advantage of Raymond, but Zock is able to protect his friend by pretending to be ill. Because the boys love and understand each other and because Zock is always there to protect Raymond from the dangers of his ignorance, their intentions are rarely disproportionate to reality.

In Chicago, Raymond and Zock see the movie *Gunga Din* three times and are deeply affected by its treatment of sacrificial death. Because Gunga Din's devotion to the British soldiers and the civilization they represent symbolizes the devotion and deep affection Raymond and Zock share, the water carrier becomes a heroic model for the boys to worship and emulate. For Raymond, however, Gunga Din is more than a symbol of friendship. He is a person whose good intentions are congruent with reality. The life bearer wants to save the lives of the troops and he does. He is killed in the process, but because he knows that he is going to die, reality cannot confuse him. He cannot be both a success and a failure. Gunga Din's death symbolizes a victory of intention over reality and lends credence to Raymond's unconscious belief that innocence, hope, and idealism can triumph without being accompanied by guilt and disillusionment.

In an attempt to share the friendship they have found, to be life bearers like Gunga Din, Raymond and Zock make friends with a black brawny poetry lover named Felix Brown. Raymond, Zock, and Felix become something of a threesome, but their relationship is short-lived. Zock's father, a haberdasher, blames the drop-off in his business on the new company that his son is keeping, and Mr. Trevitt gives Raymond a similar talk, but for different reasons. The result is Felix's embitterment toward whites and his escape from the friendship denied him in the town of Athens. Raymond and Zock, in turn, realize the hurt that their innocent, well-intentioned gestures have caused Felix, their parents, and themselves. Love, then, for Raymond and Zock, does not conquer all. A delicate emotion, the most noble action of which is sacrifice, love must be protected if it is to survive.

As a consequence of the hurt inflicted upon them by their parents, Raymond and Zock withdraw into their own private communion, which is characterized by a refined personal, unsexualized love for each other. The contrast between the adult world of Athens and the private world of Raymond and Zock is a microcosm of the larger society. Adults are aware of death and consequently appreciate the value of living, but they often reject love, the only cohesive principle upon which a sane society can be based, and replace it with ambition. The love that Zock and Raymond share must therefore be abandoned or at least reshaped if the two boys are ever going to mature into adulthood. Hence, it is little wonder that Raymond endeavors to prolong their idealistic innocence through the throes of maturation.

An important part of Raymond's initiatory process, but one that is not integral either to the plot or to any of the themes presented in *The Temple of Gold*, is Raymond's sexual awakening. When Helen Twilly graduates from college, she stops in at the Trevitt home to say good-bye to her former piano student before leaving Athens. After reminiscing about Raymond's aversion to piano lessons, Helen approaches the high school sophomore, who leads her to his upstairs bedroom. "She sat down on the bed, smiling, and then she lay all the way back, stretching her arms toward me. I didn't move. She sat up again, reached out her hands, taking me gently, guiding me over to the bed. Pretty soon everything was warm and soft and neither of us was shaking anymore" (p. 41).[1]

Like Sherwood Anderson, F. Scott Fitzgerald, Ernest Hemingway, and other good writers who have dealt with sexual initiation, Goldman realizes the seriousness of the act to those participating and refuses to make it comical, unimportant, or freakish. Important as it may be, however, Raymond's sexual awakening is not a part of his initiation into adulthood. It is a pleasant learning experience, but falls short of being an adult ordeal or crisis. Adult confirmation in the world, Goldman seems to be saying, comes not through sex, or even love, but through a painful realization of death and the recognition of how important it is to be alive. Until that time comes, however, Raymond continues to look to his friendship with Zock or somewhere else, like the local bar, to escape the recognition of reality that constitutes real maturity.

When Zock returns home from Harvard for a vacation, Raymond invites his protector to join him for a drink. Driving home from the local bar, Raymond loses control of the car, but before it crashes into Half Day Bridge, Zock tells Raymond, "The temple of gold, Euripides. The temple of gold" (p. 93). Raymond is thrown from the car and escapes injury, but Zock, who is trapped at the point of impact, dies. Four days later, Raymond joins the army.

Considering that within the book's first eighty-five pages, Raymond kills his father's guppies, breaks up a faculty wives' meeting, receives his first and only beating, goes through three schools, runs away to Chicago, is seduced by his former piano teacher, falls in love twice, and enlists in the army four days after causing the death of his best friend, the reader may see Raymond's search for adulthood as nothing more than a physical rampage through society. This may be true, but Raymond's lack of critical self-consciousness only confirms his innocent adolescence and the danger it poses to others. Furthermore, Raymond's decision to escape his home life, which by its very nature can hardly be worse than army life, dramatizes the degree of his ignorance and his desperate desire to protect it from maturity.

By having Raymond enlist in the army so soon after Zock's death, Goldman establishes two important points. Raymond's desire to avoid reflection and confrontation demonstrates the parity that exists between innocence and its destructive nature. He knows no more about army life than he did about feeding his father's guppies and the dangers of alcohol. Second, Raymond's enlistment further demonstrates the disparity between his intentions and his experiences.

Raymond finds the army to be more difficult than civilian life, but somehow his escape from the responsibilities that confronted him in Athens has provided him with the opportunity to mature in Camp Scott. When Zock's father visits him, Raymond admits his responsibility in the young man's death, and comforts Mr. Crowe, when he breaks down, by telling him that Zock's last words were that he loved his father. Raymond's maturity in military matters and in his treatment of Mr. Crowe, as well as his reflections on his responsibility for Zock's death, indicates his willingness to enter adulthood. However, Raymond's inability to discover the meaning of the actual words that Zock spoke before he died ("The temple of gold, Euripides") shows that Raymond still has a long way to go in the initiatory process.

Through the death of Ulysses S. Kelly, a friend he meets in the army, Raymond learns that he cannot escape the desctructive elements of his innocence or make his intentions coincide with reality. The son of a chief of staff, Ulysses is trying unsuccessfully to be the kind of soldier his father wants him to be and turns to Raymond for support. Naively believing that women and liquor will prove attractive enough to make Ulysses buck his father's ambition and discover life on his own, Raymond offers them to his friend as alternatives to military achievement. Recognizing the truth of what Raymond is demonstrating, but unable to act against his father's stronger will, Ulysses kills himself.

After his discharge from the army, Raymond returns to Athens and has one of his rare conversations with his father. Making a pretentious analogy between Raymond and Christ in the Garden of Gethsemane, Professor Trevitt admits having failed his son in his hour of need and asks him to recognize failure as a part of life about which nothing can be done. Not wanting to accept his having failed Zock, Ulysses, or his parents, or their having failed him, Raymond runs once again from Athens. When he gets to Cambridge, he reads the news of his father's unexpected death in the obituary column of the *New York Times*. Through his father's death, Raymond realizes that his past is an inescapable part of him. He is ever in the presence of his own essence. Instead of being able to look forward to tomorrow and life, Raymond must look back into yesterday and death.

From the point of Raymond's realization that he cannot escape his past, *The Temple of Gold* begins to falter. The interesting themes established in the early stages of the book and the paradoxes presented in its middle sections become deflated in the novel's final stages by a contrived plot. The ultimate responsibility for the book's faltering lies with Goldman, but a sharer of that responsibility is the Alfred A. Knopf Publishing Company, which requested that Goldman add a hundred pages after Ulysses' suicide.

After missing his father's funeral, Raymond cloisters himself in his room for ten months and reads every book in his father's library. Except for a double date with his mother and her boyfriend, Adrian Baugh, and a day at the lake with his first girlfriend, Harriet, the only time Raymond leaves his books is when he goes to Crystal City and marries Terry Clark, a local prostitute. Shortly afterwards, in an apparent attempt to be responsible, Raymond enters Athens College and joins the staff of the literary magazine. His ambition to be its editor, however, is blocked by Professor Janes, who resents Raymond for once having taken sexual advantage of his student-lover, Annabelle. Disappointed by Professor Janes's decision to appoint someone else as editor, Raymond returns home to attend his mother's wedding to Adrian Baugh. There he discovers that his wife is having an affair with their sixteen-year-old neighbor, Andy Peabody. Raymond immediately throws Terry out of the house, leaves the wedding, gets drunk, and spends the night sleeping on Zock's grave. The next day, he tells Andy Peabody, "Everybody fails. Everybody fails everybody. Just like God. God failed. God failed his own son in the Garden of Gethsemane" (p. 182).

Repeating his father's speech to Andy, however, does not symbolize Raymond's having entered into maturity as his reactions to Professor Janes, whom he unsuccessfully tries to blackmail, and to Terry, whom he throws out of his house without recognizing his neglect of her, aptly demonstrate. Raymond has reached the borderline of maturity, but he has not crossed it. In speech, in temperament, and in his reactions to what he experiences, Raymond is still an adolescent: ". . . you were wrong, Zock. There isn't any handle, any temple of gold" (p. 194). Until he learns to recognize death as a part of a pattern and appreciate the value of living by taking his place in the adult world, Raymond will continue to be a youth whose innocence represents a threat to the adult community.

The reader's appreciation of the events in Raymond's life is heightened by the protagonist's self-conscious narrative role, which creates a powerful tension between the magnitude of his suffering and the incapacity of his adolescent language. Carefully controlled by Goldman, Raymond's language is the instrument that, more than any other, gives the novel its strong sense of real life, and makes its plot almost entirely believable on first reading. When, with an innocence of his own, Goldman says things that are not true, he is nevertheless believable because of the emotion his language conveys. For example, when talking about the meaningful conversations he has enjoyed with Zock, Raymond says, "We talked about ourselves, free and open, like a Catholic at confession, not hiding anything but just speaking our minds" (p. 30). Goldman has obviously never been to confession, a sacrament of fear, guilt, and penance, but he conveys the emotion that exists between Raymond and Zock almost well enough to escape the reader's wondering whether he has.

Paralleling the dramatic tension in *The Temple of Gold* is a philosophical one. Raymond is trapped in two overlapping worlds. In one exists the beautiful but impossible ideals of Zock and Gunga Din; in the other is man's inescapable reality. By the end of his story, Raymond announces his failure to find a place in the adult world that will accept his innocent ideals. From a social position similar to that of Salinger's Holden Caulfield at the end of *Catcher in the Rye*, Raymond echoes the resolution of his other prototype, Mark Twain's Huckleberry Finn, to "light out of the territory": "I'm taking off and don't ask me where, because I don't know. But there's a lot of places I haven't been, but I've been here" (p. 184).

While *The Temple of Gold* fails to initiate Raymond Trevitt into adulthood, it does furnish him with a set of experiences that increases his knowledge of adult life. His final position in the novel, then, may also be Goldman's. The young writer has discovered his strengths to lie in the interesting characters that he develops and the colloquial style that offers credibility of his story, but his dependence on a contrived plot has hindered his reaching writing maturity with his first novel. Goldman's immaturity as a writer, however, does not mean that *The Temple of Gold* is necessarily an immature piece of fiction. The stories about adolescence that are immature are those that condescendingly describe their heroes from the superior point of view of an adult. The adventures of Tom Sawyer, for example, often seem somewhat ridiculous because they are motivated by those confusions of adolescence that their adult author outgrew. Novels that are genuinely mature, such as *The Adventures of Huckleberry Finn* and *Catcher in the Rye*, enter into the lives of their adolescents at first hand, and describe them through the eyes of their protagonists. Hence, *The Temple of Gold* may be seen as a significant achievement for a first novel and its inexperienced author.

The interesting characters, important themes, and narrative techniques which Goldman established in *The Temple of Gold*, he continued to improve upon in subsequent novels. For example, he learned from his first book that it is not important to account for all his novel's characters in the concluding chapter. Had *The Temple of Gold* not been Goldman's first work, it seems safe to say that Raymond would not have had to throw his wife out of the house so that he could then go and look for her and run into Felix Brown in Crystal City. Felix's role in the novel sensibly ended when he left Athens in bitterness caused by Raymond's and Zock's betrayal of his friendship.

Goldman also improves upon the narrative tricks he plays on his readers. When Raymond marries a prostitute, the reader is disappointed because Goldman has led him to believe that the protagonist would marry the likable Harriet. Furthermore, Goldman never offers an explanation for Raymond's marrying Terry, and none of the traditional reasons for marriage apply here. In his subsequent novels, Goldman continues to play sleight-of-hand narrative tricks, but his readers are not disappointed because the books' plots are made believable by the characters their author has created.

Relying on protagonists who speak dialogue so believable that one is almost inclined not to think twice about their actions, Goldman maintains the reader's interest throughout the early novels. However, by failing to write novels whose plots are free of obvious contrivance, Goldman retarded his development as a writer.

CHAPTER 3

Avoiding Reality: Your Turn to Curtsy, My Turn to Bow

THAT Goldman was in no hurry to reach writing maturity is evidenced by his spending the first fifty weeks after the publication of *The Temple of Gold* doing little more than watching movies. Within the fifty-first week, however, Goldman wrote his second novel, *Your Turn to Curtsy, My Turn to Bow* (1958). The book, according to Gregory McDonald, who wrote its first review in 1966 for the *Boston Globe*, has "a fresh idea but one is inclined to think Mr. Goldman, perhaps in the panic of despair, perhaps because it was something from the trunk, anyway, perhaps because he felt he had to have a second book out quickly, did not develop and polish it enough to fully realize its potential. It was slight and used a religious imagery some might feel immature. Yet it had the wonderful, rare spontaneity of youth and a few memorable scenes."

Your Turn to Curtsy, My Turn to Bow does have a "fresh idea," but its "creative genesis," as Goldman would say, is an old one. "That book began with a story by Harold Brodkey in the *New Yorker* called 'First Love,' and I thought, 'I can write a better love story.' I don't remember if I sat down to write it then or a year later, but the creative genesis of *Your Turn to Curtsy, My Turn to Bow* was to write a romantic story. It's a love story, but it's not a romance. How from a summer romance I wound up with a guy who crucifies himself, I don't know" (WG).

Because *Your Turn to Curtsy, My Turn to Bow* developed from a love story into a tale of initiation, it invites comparison with *The Temple of Gold* rather than with Brodkey's narrative. The protagonist of Goldman's second novel is like Raymond Trevitt of *The Temple of Gold* in that he loses a close friend and fails to reach maturity. Unlike Raymond, however, Peter Bell has no desire to protect his innocence.

35

In spite of the fact that he is willing to suffer the loss of his ingenuousness, the central conflict of Peter's life is still between innocence and experience. Because he has few ideas about what adulthood involves, Peter's confrontations with adult realities, like Raymond's, are painful. Although he has Raymond's almost saintly capacity for pain, Peter lacks the corresponding criminal passion for heresy. Tempered by a knowledge that comes from books, Peter's innocence causes pain, but it is not dangerous.

Shortly after his arrival at Camp Blackpine, where he will be working as a summer counselor, Peter Bell meets Tillie Keck, the camp secretary's niece. He is so attracted to her that he falls immediately in love, but she does not return his affection. She swims and sunbathes with him and occasionally walks into town with him for lunch, but she reserves her evenings and apparently her affection for Peter's sensible but impersonal supervisor, Granny Kemp.

Peter's failure to make Tillie reciprocate his affection marks the first time that Goldman presents his theme of unfulfilled or thwarted intentions through a direct confrontation. When, in *The Temple of Gold,* Raymond confronts this frustration, he retreats into the protection that his relationship with Zock affords. When Zock is no longer around, he retreats to the army, Cambridge, school, marriage, drink, or whatever other conventional escapes he thinks will protect him from adulthood. In *Your Turn to Curtsy, My Turn to Bow,* however, Goldman's protagonist recognizes the frustration and pain of being ignorant and yearns to gain the experience that will enable him to compete with Granny for Tillie's love.

The love that Tillie does not give to Peter is offered to him instead by Chad Kimberly, a local athletic hero, who has a Christ-fixation and whom Peter has worshipped since he was in the seventh grade. Goldman's model for Chad Kimberly is Hobie Baker, an Ivy League athletic hero, who also won fame during World War I. "Hobie Baker was the greatest athlete in the history of Princeton University. He was a football star and a blond, and was probably the greatest hockey player that ever lived. He was such a phenomenal hockey player, that Princeton, an Ivy League school, would come to the Garden and there would be headlines that would say, 'Hobie Baker Plays at the Garden Tonight.' And the Garden would sell out. He never turned pro because World War I came. He did all right in World War I. He was a flyer. On the day of the armistice, he took up a plane and flew it into the ground. It had been so glorious for him that the idea of the war ending and going back and just making a lot of money on Wall

Street was just so terrible that he went mad and killed himself. He was one of the most glorified creatures to ever happen" (WG).[1]

Although Chad's athletic career does not measure up to Hobie Baker's, his end is more dramatic than flying a plane into the ground. As Goldman says, "If the book works at all, it does so on the belief that Chad is so loony that he will crucify himself. Now, if he has to crucify himself, he has to think he's Christ. He has to have Christ-like experiences. Peter is his disciple, and all that occurred with him is to justify Chad's madness."

Because they are both objects of Peter's affection and because he is forced to make a choice between them, a comparison of Tillie and Chad is important for a better understanding of the novel. Of Tillie Peter says, "It was looking at her that did it. Just looking at her. Standing, sitting, walking around her, glancing at her from the side, from the front, almost hopefully trying to find some flaw lurking hidden in her flawless face. He found none" (pp. 32–33).[2]

Peter's love for Tillie is paralleled by his worship of Chad. In both cases, Peter is too inexperienced in life to admit any faults in the people he loves. If he enjoys looking at Tillie, so too does Peter take pleasure in spying on Chad, who is four years his senior. "Occasionally, during college vacations, Chad would revisit the high school and Peter would follow him, staring, . . . watching the tall blonde boy and the crowd of young men who always surrounded him. . . . Probably an outsider would have termed it a common case of hero worship. But Peter Bell thought it was more" (pp. 47–48).

Tillie and Chad are physically superior people and Peter is sexually attracted to them both, but Tillie's beauty is tainted by a provincialism that Peter does not recognize as a drawback. Because of her limited social background, Tillie has to read "a crappy thing on manners" to find out what kind of utensil an "outside spoon" is. She does not know the meaning of the word "gauche," spells "Pygmalion" as if it were two words, the first one being "pig," and is more interested in getting an even tan than in meaningful conversation with Peter. Peter, who is smarter but even more inexperienced than Tillie, allows his adoration of her to distort his perception. Hence, he misses his chance to play Professor Higgins and loses Tillie every night to the boorish Granny.

Chad's beauty, on the other hand, becomes either enhanced or tainted, depending on the viewpoint through which he is seen. Granny thinks Chad is crazy and is wary of him. Peter is homosexually attracted to Chad as Chad is to him, yet Peter's awe of his idol approaches that of Raymond and Zock for Gunga Din. The love, affection, and understanding that Chad and Peter give to each other mark the most tender moments of the novel. However, Chad's unreasonable insistence that his disciple follow him without question harms them both.

Confusedly adopting the personality of the demanding Old Testament God with the loving ethic of the New Testament Christ, Chad provides the higher, personal, and latently homosexual though not untouching love that Zock shared with Raymond. Yet the demands that Chad makes on Peter are, in fact, basically unloving. They recognize Peter's status as a disciple but fail to respect his integrity as a person.

Chad's ambiguous psychological development from football hero to Christ-figure may strain some reader's capacities for identification, but his seeking refuge from adult realities through his belief that he is Christ does contain elements of psychological truth.[3] Peter, on the other hand, yearns to confront the adult world and resents Chad's trying to keep him from it. Considering their love, separate desires, and Chad's demands, a confrontation between the two latent lovers is inevitable.

Thrilled by Tillie's finally consenting to spend an evening with him, Peter asks Chad to suggest a place where he might take her. Chad, however, tells his disciple that he does not want him to see Tillie, and, like the God of the Old Testament, expects Peter to obey his unreasonable command without question. Because Chad will not furnish a reason for his advice, Peter resolves to be with Tillie.

On their date, which is spent canoeing on Lake Cherokee, Peter is nervous about making a good impression on Tillie. His conversation is awkward and reveals his anxiety, but Tillie, who seems to sense this, is polite to him. When they hear music coming from a dance that is being held in the town, Peter tells Tillie about an experience he had on his first day of dancing school. "The craziest thing happened. . . . She lined us up in two long rows, facing each other. And then she signaled the piano player . . . and he started pounding away. And then she began moving around, . . . And all the time she walked, she kept saying, 'Your turn to curtsy, my turn to bow,' and she'd gesture for us to do the same thing. . . . Don't you see? We were just little kids. We didn't know what she was talking about. We didn't know who was supposed to curtsy and who was supposed to bow" (p. 81).

Peter's situation in the canoe is similar to the experience in his dancing class. "Indiscriminately virginal," Peter does not know his role in relationships with women. Later, when Peter takes Tillie back to her cabin at the camp, she puts her arms around him and kisses him good night. Excited by Tillie's kiss, Peter runs to tell Chad what an enjoyable evening he has had. Before he reaches his friend's cabin, however, he is met by Granny, who tells Peter that Tillie went out with him in order to settle a bet made among the camp counselors: "We just wanted to see if you'd score, that's all. The rest of us have. I said you wouldn't (p. 86).

Humiliated by his sexual inexperience being the object of a bet and by Tillie's deceiving him, Peter retreats to the private glen where he and Chad share intimate conversations. Like the private chapel in Stephen Crane's *The Red Badge of Courage*, Chad and Peter's glen gives the boys a feeling that is half religious: "Everything seemed soft to him; the pine needle floor of the wood, the sky, the moon, the yellow-topped lake, they all seemed to meld and melt into a great taffy-textured landscape, . . . He had no idea of time or place, but only of soft things, of water and sky and thick carpeted earth" (pp. 35–36).

The respective chapels, however, are not retreats from the world. In Henry Fleming's, the corpse of the dead soldier lies staring at whoever enters. In Peter Bell's, there occurs the confrontation between the Christ-figure and his disciple that eventually leads Chad to his cross. When Chad admits that he knew all along about Granny's bet but did not tell Peter because he wanted to teach the disciple a lesson, Goldman's young protagonist runs to Tillie's cottage, where he barges in on her to tell her that he once loved her. Tillie responds by leading Peter into her bed and initiating him into sexual knowledge.

In spite of the rather extraordinary events leading up to his first sexual experience, Peter's losing his virginity is much more integral to the novel's plot than Raymond's is in *The Temple of Gold*. Raymond's coupling with Helen Twilly, his former piano teacher, is an important aspect of Raymond's adolescence, but its only effect on the narrative is to lengthen it. Peter's sexual awakening, on the other hand, not only brings his relationship with Tillie to a climax, but it also contrasts with the kind of love Peter shares with Chad. What Goldman seems to be saying here is the communion that can exist between males is a higher form of love than that found in male-female relationships. If this is true, it is Goldman's deficiency as a novelist that the women with whom his adolescent protagonists enter into

sexual affairs are so intellectually and socially inferior that the
possibilities of a meaningful relationship are almost totally negated.

Betrayed by what he interprets as Peter's disloyalty to him as a
Christ-figure and sexually rejected in favor of Tillie, Chad nails his
feet and left hand to a cross at the campfire ring. When Peter
discovers him, Chad asks his disciple to hammer a final nail through
his unpierced hand. Instead, Peter takes his pathetic friend down
from the cross, and, after Chad is hospitalized, returns him to his
family in Athens.

Because he is limited by Peter's unperceptive point of view, the
reader has little information regarding the initial causes of Chad's
schizophrenia. Consequently, he has trouble believing Goldman's
ambiguous presentation of self-aggression. Nevertheless, the
Christ-figure's crucifixion may be interpreted as an attack on himself
as a product of the irreconcilable struggle between man and society as
well as an act designed to make his unfaithful disciple feel guilty.[4]
Because Goldman does not offer a clear picture of what Chad's primal
roots might be, however, any demonstration of what may possibily be
interpreted as a masochistic ego choosing to achieve victory in defeat as
incomprehensible and consequently lacks credibility.

At the time Peter is telling his story, he is twenty-seven years of
age, and no longer thirsts for adult experiences. His life is quiet and
much of his time is spent trying to forget his initiation and the boy he
thinks he was at Camp Blackpine. Like Nick Carraway of F. Scott
Fitzgerald's *The Great Gatsby*, Peter Bell represents the traditional
moral codes of America, perceives the essential pathos of the hero he
worships, and, at the novel's end, lives in a present that continually
reminds him of his past.

Similarly, as Jay Gatsby is the subject of Carraway's narrative, so
too is Chad Kimberly the subject of Peter's. Both are dramatic
symbols of an idealism that turns reality into a kind of romantic
expectation, which inevitably leads to disappointment. The essence
of their tragedies, however, lies not in Jay's death or in Chad's return
to the sanitarium, but rather in the waste of their enormous energies
and in their sacrifices to self-illusion. As Nick perceives the essential
pathos of Jay Gatsby's romantic idealism, so too does Peter's perception of Chad's idealistic love set him and his hero apart from the carnal
Granny Kemper and the opportunistic Tillie Keck. Nick and Peter
understand that their heroes are motivated not by the selfishness that
characterizes the other people in the novels but by their devotion to

an ideal that has been rendered false by the moral vacuum of East Egg and Camp Blackpine.

Although Goldman's Christ-figure may appear somewhat melodramatic or even a regression from his first novel,[5] *Your Turn to Curtsy, My Turn to Bow* continues to develop relevant issues such as the reassessment of innocence as a symbol of true insight, the disproportion between man's intentions and reality, the seriousness of sexual awakenings, the importance of personalized communion between friends, latent homosexuality, the search for a protector in male relationships, and the internalization of the knowledge of death as a necessary step in the initiatory process. In addition, Goldman's second novel introduces the theme of man as a self-destructive force. In spite of the well-drawn characters and realistic dialogue that convey these themes, however, *Your Turn to Curtsy, My Turn to Bow* falls short of reaching a level of mature fiction on the ground that Goldman has failed to effectively relate what he is saying to how he is saying it.

Chad's crucifixion in *Your Turn to Curtsy, My Turn to Bow*, like Zock's death in *The Temple of Gold*, is an ineffective correlative. When, in his first novel, Goldman uses Gunga Din as a symbol of Zock and Raymond's friendship, he presents a well-chosen model for the boys to emulate but one whose death is far more significant than Zock's. Whereas Gunga Din's death increases his friends' sense of human appreciation and saves British civilization in India, Zock's death neither civilizes Raymond nor saves others from his recklessness. Similarly, as painful as the sexual rejection and philosophical betrayal which Chad suffers may be, they are ordinary experiences and simply do not warrant a melodramatic suicide attempt. Because he fails to furnish an adequate justification for Chad's crucifixion, Goldman loses his reader's willingness to identify with his Christ-figure's plight.

Goldman's use of the dancing class, on the other hand, is an effective correlative. It adequately symbolizes the social ignorance that Peter displays in the canoe with Tillie and indicates Peter's desire to escape adult reality by dreaming of his untainted youth. Like Nick Carraway, Peter Bell has had enough "privileged glimpses into the human heart," and now wants "the world to be in uniform and at a sort of moral attention forever."[6] Reflecting Peter's desire for this sort of moral regimentation are the novel's final lines: "And so it's your turn to curtsy, my turn to bow, your turn to curtsy, now mine,

you, now me, on and on, until one of the dancers falls, I suppose, or
until the dance is ended . . ." (p. 116). Rhythmically, Peter's words
echo Nick's final sentiment: "So we beat on, boats against the current,
borne back ceaselessly into the past." Says Goldman about the
concluding lines of his novel, "It's a strange book, but is has a
wonderful sentence at the end. I don't write that well, and if I get a
good sentence, I remember it. I love that one."

In spite of his inability to create consistently successful correla-
tives, Goldman's development as a writer does improve from his first
to his second book. His ability to organize and narrate a variety of
details and characters through a point of view that continually shifts
from first to third person foreshadows the exciting structural ac-
complishments of his later novels. The individual stories of Peter and
Tillie, like those of Raymond and Zock in *The Temple of Gold*, are put
together exceptionally well and further demonstrate Goldman's
near-perfect ear for spoken language.

A narrative device introduced by Goldman in *Your Turn to Curtsy,
My Turn to Bow* is the projection of future scenes in the novel into the
early stages of the narrative. On his first day at camp, Peter is relaxing
by the swimming pool when he hears a voice.

"Look out if you don't want to get splashed."
Peter rolled over and opened his eyes. . . . Tillie Keck was beautiful. She
was exquisite but not to his eyes alone. For on the afternoon of the day they
met, as they were strolling through the town of Cherokee, an old man, . . .
blocked their path. Then without a word, he slowly touched his fingers to her
skin . . . .
"Lookout," she called again. "You'll get splashed." (pp. 18–21)

Goldman's reversal of the flashback makes the reader wonder
what connection exists between the old man and the young couple.
Several pages after it is first mentioned, the incident is repeated
within its chronological context. The repetition serves not only to
heighten the reader's interest in the narrative and emphasize the
importance of the scene to Peter Bell but also to introduce the story of
Tillie's almost being raped at the age of sixteen by her stepfather.
Flashforwards such as this one mark Goldman's first use of cinematic
techniques in his writing.[8] In subsequent books, he will combine this
with other film techniques to alter significantly the traditional form of
the novel.

Your Turn to Curtsy, My Turn to Bow, obviously a book of
transition, employs the close first-person narrative of *The Temple of*

Gold as well as the third-person technique that Goldman employs in each of his subsequent novels. Even though Goldman's second novel was not reviewed when it was published, the book strangely has enjoyed more than fourteen printings in paperback. As Goldman points out, "Doubleday published it because they thought I might make some money for them someday, but the book found a certain cult. It's sold a lot of copies, and it's very popular with the kids in the high schools and colleges. It's a very strange thing."

The Temple of Gold and *Your Turn to Curtsy, My Turn to Bow*, then, are stories about two boys who lose their innocence but fail to enter adulthood. Raymond Trevitt escapes from his adult responsibilities by running away from Athens; Peter Bell protects himself from maturity by dreaming about the days of his innocent youth. Their creator was an improved writer when he finished his second novel, but he had yet to reach the level of a mature one.

The popular books written today about immature boys (Salinger's Holden Caulfield, Goldman's Raymond Trevitt and Peter Bell, and James Kirkwood's Peter Kilburn of *Good Times/Bad Times*) may be more of a comment about young readers than about their authors' narrative abilities. Nevertheless, Goldman's early novels about escape and madness offer readers of all ages good stories about young people trying to protect themselves from a world with which they are unprepared to cope. In his later novels, as we shall observe, Goldman offers a mature and complex commentary upon escapism and at best perhaps a way of rising above the inexorable realm of everyday reality to a higher ground from which the necessity and pain of life continues to be understood in human terms.

CHAPTER 4

Coping with Reality: Soldier in the Rain

I write very quickly, and I don't take notes, and I remember thinking with *Soldier in the Rain* that I would limit myself to five pages a day. I did that for the first four chapters of that book, and then I got stuck. I gave the book to a friend of mine, John Kander, the composer for *Cabaret* and *Chicago*. He was a roommate of mine and so was my brother. We all lived together for several years in the beginning. I said to John, 'I'm stuck. What do I do?' At this point it was just a bunch of stories about an army post. That was the only narrative. And John said, 'Gee, I thought that girl was fun. Why don't you bring back the girl?' When he said that, I thought, 'Yes, I'll bring back the girl, and I'll put her with the fat sergeant,' and all of a sudden, I had the rest of the book. I went back to my home in Chicago, and I wrote the last one hundred and fifty pages of the book in a week" (WG).

Soldier in the Rain (1960)[1] was published one year before ex-pilot Joseph Heller dropped his first literary bombshell; and, like *Catch 22* it confused and wounded the sensibilities of many early reviewers. The *New York Times* complained that the book was "a city novelists's version of a Tennessee ridge-runner"; *Library Journal's* C. W. Mann exclaimed that Goldman had "finished the book as if he were shaking something out of his craw"; and Bosley Crowther of the *Times* insisted that the 1962 film adaptation, which Goldman did not write, was "neither good knockabout comedy nor trustworthy sentimental drama."

Unwittingly, Crowther's statement comes close to explaining much of the early criticism against Goldman's novel. Because it concerned the noncombatant aspects of military life, *Soldier in the Rain* was more often than not judged on the same terms as the then-popular television show, *Sergeant Bilko*, when, in fact, the novel is anything but a situation comedy. Although riddled with sentimentalism, *Soldier in the Rain*, at its core, is like *Catch 22* in that it uses the army as a metaphor to protest against institutions that usurp man's power over his own life.

In *The Temple of Gold* and *Your Turn to Curtsy, My Turn to Bow*, the chaos of the adult world signifies a loss of innocence that Raymond Trevitt and Peter Bell equate with a loss of humanity. By encountering and then escaping from the process that initiates young people into maturity, Raymond and Peter suffer the loss of their innocence but manage to affirm their humanity without becoming adults. In *Soldier in the Rain*, however, the military institution usurps its members' right to encounter the chaos of adulthood and thereby prevents them from discovering a way to affirm their lives. This may well be the reason why Raymond, in *The Temple of Gold*, is so gung ho during his basic training period at Camp Scott. As long as he substitutes the army's rationale for the one he brought with him, he successfully escapes from the chaos he fled in Athens. Conversely, as soon as Raymond rejects military ideals and begins to sympathize with the plight of his friend, Ulysses, he finds himself confronting the very issue of adult responsibility from which he had hoped to escape.

Soldier in the Rain is the meandering story of Eustis Clay, a semi-illiterate supply sergeant, his two hundred and fifty pound protector, Maxwell Slaughter, and Clay's protégé, Jerry Meltzer, a drafted graduate from Yale University. Eustis, like Raymond and Peter of *The Temple of Gold* and *Your Turn to Curtsy, My Turn to Bow*, respectively, has reached full physical maturity and is no longer an innocent, but his powers of imagination, reason, and judgment are dependent on the learning and experience of Maxwell, who does the *Times* crossword puzzle in ink and is the only noncommissioned officer at Camp Scott to have his own soft-drink machine and air conditioner. Together, these three musketeers exploit the military bureaucracy for their own benefit while they are unconsciously being victimized by it.

Even though *Soldier in the Rain* takes place during the Korean War, the book is not about fighting. Much like *Mister Roberts*, Thomas Heggen's novel of the World War II navy, Goldman's novel concerns the establishment that runs the war and uses it to destroy the enemy at home as well as the one abroad. By destroying the sanity and spirit of its soldiers, the army is able to produce an organized body of nonhumans who substitute the values of the institution for reason and righteousness. In the sense that *Soldier in the Rain* attacks an establishment whose bureaucracy negates life under the guise of rational order, Goldman's novel foreshadows many of the radical protest novels that appeared throughout the sixties.

Its structural looseness, poorly integrated ending, and indulgence in further developing the themes presented in Goldman's first novels prevent *Soldier in the Rain* from producing the social impact of books such as *Catch 22* (1961) or Ken Kesey's *One Flew Over the Cuckoo's Nest* (1962). Nevertheless, Goldman's book about affirming life within institutions that negate it is representative of a number of important novels of this genre. Unlike Heller's Yossarian, who runs from the institution, or Kesey's McCurphy, who confronts it, Goldman's characters attempt to make their lives comfortable by dealing with it, by giving a little of themselves to get in return a little of what good things the army has to offer. Mostly everyone scratches everyone else's back, but what they get in return amounts to nothing more than a fan, six mattresses, twelve pairs of cotton underwear with elastic waists, clean sheets, an air conditioner, a set of golf clubs, free grape soda, and the one-hour use of a truck whose gas tank is empty. Because love and understanding have no place in the institution, they are rarely experienced. The result is material profit and comfort for some but meaningless activity and degradation for everyone else.

As soon as Clay sets up in his room a fan that Maxwell no longer needs, it is arbitrarily confiscated by Captain Magee. To get the fan back from Captain Magee, Eustis pretends to be suffering from "scabosis," a fictitious disease attributed to overworked sweat glands. Maxwell, impersonating Major-Doctor Schmidt, confirms Clay's plea that the fan is necessary for his cure. The fan is returned to Clay's room, but it does not remain there for long. Clay's nemesis, Sergeant Priest, finds out about a mattress sale that Goldman's protagonist made to Maxwell and makes Clay bribe him with the fan in order to avoid a complete investigation of the sergeant's supply room.

By paying its members a wage that prevents them from acquiring luxuries of any kind, the army forces it soldiers to rely on the institution for their comforts. Economically deprived and consequently somewhat depraved, the soldiers must make do with whatever exists at Camp Scott. Furthermore, by forcing its members to concentrate a significant amount of their time and energy on acquiring material goods, the institution succeeds in keeping life's more important issues separate from the lives of its members. As long as Eustis concentrates on his fan and Maxwell on his underwear, neither thinks about the indirect role he plays in the deaths of many Americans and Koreans. The army's economic system, then, is a microcosm as well as a part of the greater institution known as America, where immediate gratification through material goods is of foremost importance.

The economic system also serves the military machine by refusing to recognize the principles of friendship. Maxwell, who is supposed to be a protector-figure as well as a close friend, forces Clay to contract a business agreement that jeopardizes his position as supply sergeant. The sacredness of friendship, which eventually drives Raymond and Felix from Athens in *The Temple of Gold* and Chad to the cross in *Your Turn to Curtsy, My Turn to Bow*, becomes replaced by the profit motive in *Soldier in the Rain*. Eustis, who breaks down at the news of his dog's death, is totally insensitive to Maxwell's placing underwear, mattresses, and clean windows above their friendship because Eustis, too, considers these items to be of prime importance. By devoting their energies to material comforts, Eustis and Maxwell keep their relationship from ever reaching the personalized, intimate level of the friendship enjoyed by the protagonists in Goldman's first two novels.

The basic inhumanity of the military-economic institution is further preserved by its pecking order. Captain Magee wants Eustis's fan; his higher rank permits him to take it. Magee returns the fan to Eustis not for reasons of the supply sergeant's health but because Major Schmidt orders him to do so. When Eustis needs men to clean Maxwell's office and cut his grass, he turns to the recruits, who are the only people he can command. What is commanded, then, is right simply because it is commanded.

Because the institution has replaced man's control over his own life with a chain of command, there is little justice for any of its individual members. Eustis is given a long-awaited three-day pass to attend the Kentucky Derby, but the pass is revoked when a surprise inspection reveals the supply sergeant's untidy room. When the drunk Corporal Lenehan drives his car into the rear end of the car Eustis is driving, Sergeant Priest comes to Lenehan's defense and tries to have the innocent Eustis and his friend Meltzer jailed for the misdemeanor of which Lenehan is guilty.

Meltzer, who lacks Eustis's six years of army experience, can only offer helpless gestures to the judgments being administered by the court. The protégé's inertness is partially due to the beer he has been drinking, but it is also his response to a system that fails to recognize the humanity of its members. In an institution where everything leads to death, inertia, and the betrayal of humanity, it is no wonder that Goldman's characters become neurotic, petty, alienated, aimless, and bored. To sustain them, they have the loose women who frequent the camp.

Frances, who has a thirty-nine-inch bustline, is described as the only girl in the South who wears angora sweaters all year round. Bobby Jo, on the other hand, is still developing breasts. Having a noticeably limited intelligence, her sense of self comes from the flattery she receives from men. While Eustis's relationship with Frances is limited to sex, Maxwell's relationship with Bobby Jo is merely one of a sexual condescension. The forty-year-old, reasonably educated Maxwell treats Bobby Jo as the child she is and insults her by refusing her invitation to couple. Nevertheless, he gives her the attention she craves and eventually becomes her "baby boyfriend." Although it is never stated explicitly, Bobby Jo fulfills some inner need of Maxwell's and he enjoys her company almost as much as she does his.

Whether Frances and Bobby Jo are a comment on the kind of women who frequent military bases or whether they represent the only kind of women Eustis and Maxwell can attract, Goldman leaves ambiguous. However, it is probably safe to say that Frances and Bobby Jo are the kind of women Eustis and Maxwell want. Because Eustic only sees women as objects for male gratification, Frances's personality is limited to her breasts. Maxwell's interest in Bobby Jo, on the other hand, is primarily paternal. Like Raymond and Peter, in *The Temple of Gold* and *Your Turn to Curtsy, My Turn to Bow*, Eustis and Maxwell are attracted to women who are socially and intellectually their inferiors.

The only attractive woman in *Soldier in the Rain* is Meltzer's fiancee, Emmy. Raised in New York City and educated at Smith College, Emmy sees Eustis, Maxwell, and Bobby Jo for the losers they are and thinks less of Meltzer for having associated with them during his tour in the army. Described from a viewpoint sympathetic to the soldiers and Bobby Jo, however, Emmy comes off as an elitist in league with Mrs. Meltzer to protect Jerry from any experiences in life not planned by the two women. Nevertheless, Goldman's unfair treatment of her does not change the fact of Emmy's accurate insight into the dead lives led by Eustis, Maxwell, and Bobby Jo. Through

Emmy and Mrs. Meltzer, Eustis, Maxwell, and Bobby Jo realize how unsophisticated they are and prematurely leave Meltzer's reception to hasten back to Camp Scott, the only home they know and in which they can survive.

Because the institution allows its members to exist without having to develop a sense of awareness that goes beyond its borders, life outside of Camp Scott also serves to reduce human dignity. Spiritually debilitated from without as well as from within, Eustis and Maxwell eagerly return to the slower and less obvious death of the institution.

Goldman's chief concern in his early novels, however, is affirmation of life, not death. Raymond's and Peter's affirmations, in *The Temple of Gold* and *Your Turn to Curtsy, My Turn to Bow*, come about as reactions to the death of Zock and Chad's crucifixion. In *Soldier in the Rain*, however, Maxwell's suicide serves to affirm his own life, but fails to have a significant influence on Eustis. When pitted against the powers of an institution that slowly deadens its individuals' sense of humanity, each member must seize whatever opportunity is offered to gain control over his own life. Maxwell's suicide, then, constitutes more than his unwillingness to diet or give up the things he enjoys. By taking his life, Maxwell demonstrates that his existence belongs to and is ultimately determined by him, not the institution.

The events leading up to Maxwell's death begin with the death of Eustis's dog, Donald. As he did in *The Temple of Gold*, Goldman unfortunately relies upon his readers' stock responses to boys who lose their pets, and consequently fails to make Eustis's anguish over Donald's death any more credible than Raymond's distress over his dog, Baxter, or his father's guppies.

What appears a blatant sentimentalism in *The Temple of Gold*, however, becomes reduced to absurdity in *Soldier in the Rain*. Eustis's overreaction to his aunt's unfortunate news is simply not the way twenty-four-year-old men respond to the loss of pets they have not seen in years. In fact, after seeing Eustis run around Camp Scott like a madman, plead desperately for an emergency furlough, drive recklessly through the countryside, visit bars he knows he should stay out of, get drunk, and start a fight with Corporal Lenehan and Sergeant Priest, the reader is led to wonder how Eustis was ever able to leave Donald and enter the army in the first place.

Maxwell arrives at the bar in time to save Eustis from serious

injury, but he suffers a heart attack during the fight with Corporal
Lenehan and Sergeant Priest. While recuperating, Maxwell is told
that if he wants to continue living, he must lose a hundred pounds and
keep to a rigid diet thereafter. Rather than give up the only thing in
life that has ever given him real satisfaction or lose his chief sense of
individual identity, Maxwell joins Bobby Jo in a strenuous dance and
induces his fatal heart attack.

In spite of the mercenary treatment he displays toward Eustis early
in the novel and his condescension to Bobby Jo, Maxwell dies a
sympathetic character. Whenever Eustis gets into trouble, Maxwell
bails him out. He understands Eustis and cares for him, though not in
the personalized way that Goldman's other protector-figures care for
their protégés. Through his sincere interest in Bobby Jo's welfare,
Maxwell prevents the girl from getting herself into trouble with
people less sensitive to her needs and more inclined to exploit her
ignorance. For his overall kindness and sincerity, then, Maxwell can
be appreciated by the novel's readers as well as by its characters. Says
Goldman, "I tend to know before I start a book who's going to die, and
I am only able to give whatever affections I can muster as a fiction
writer to those characters that I know are going to die. That's why in
The Temple of Gold that guy dies, and that's why it's like that all the
way through my novels. Everybody dies. I don't mean that it's a trick.
It seems to be the only way I can free myself emotionally to say, 'Gee,
what a neat guy or person this person is,' is by knowing in advance
that I have to make you love them because they're going to die
because that's what life is all about. I think."

In his most recent novels, Goldman creates sympathy by telling
the reader that his heroes are going to die even when they live
beyond the last page of their narratives. The tragedy of *Soldier in the
Rain*, however, is not Maxwell's death, but rather Eustis's failure to
realize the significance of his mentor's gesture. Instead of looking to
Maxwell to learn something about life's meaning, Eustis looks up the
chain of command to the higher justice of God:

> The thunder rumbled in, but he sang on, driving faster now, swerving from
> one side of the road to the other in time with the music, listening happily,
> triumphantly, as the water sloshed around in the back seat.
> Lightning spit all around him; rain cut in at his face; thunder crashed
> against his eardrums. Another bolt of lightning, closer. Then another, closer
> still.

Clay looked up, straight up, right up into the sky.
"Fuck you," he said. (p. 248)

The novel's ending is poorly integrated into the rest of the story for two reasons. It is the first time that Eustis ever mentions or gives any indication of his belief in God. Secondly, Eustis's experiences are common and do not merit blasphemy. Consequently, the book's ending is only effective to those who consider blasphemy important and who would blaspheme under circumstances such as the ones Goldman describes.

In *The Temple of Gold*, Goldman introduces his themes of the disproportion between intention and reality, the dangers of innocence, the value of close personalized friendships, and human betrayal. In *Your Turn to Curtsy, My Turn to Bow*, these themes are placed in a summer camp setting and suffer little variation. What differences exist occur primarily in the protagonists' reactions to the events that convey Goldman's themes. In *The Temple of Gold*, Raymond runs away from the problems of Athens while Peter, in *Your Turn to Curtsy, My Turn to Bow*, escapes from the experiences of Camp Blackpine by daydreaming about the experiences of his innocent youth.

In *Soldier in the Rain*, the same themes introduced in the earlier novels are employed once more against the backdrop of an institution that plays as important a role in the book as any major character. Providing protection from the chaos of the outside world, the military-economic establishment strips its members of their humanity in order to make them serviceable. Eustis, more than any other character in the novel, symbolizes the extent to which individuals will allow an establishment to take control of their lives. Adhering to the rationale provided for him by the institution, Eustis loses the humanity to feel any emotion for Maxwell, Meltzer, Frances, or Bobby Jo, but rather reserves it for his dog. Because he cannot give enough of himself to experience the intense friendship that the protagonists of Goldman's first two novels share, Eustis cannot carry on the spirit of his protector as Raymond and Peter do. When Maxwell dies, Eustis does manage to feel a certain sense of loss and admonishes Bobby Jo for going out on a date instead of attending her "baby boyfriend's" funeral, but these feelings are soon overridden by the illusion of material success. Caught in a rainstorm that interrupts his thoughts of Maxwell and the dog, Donald, Eustis is upset by the

possible damage done to his car's upholstery. The idea of selling
portable swimming pools for cars, however, crosses his mind and
washes away the memories of those who are supposed to be closest to
him.

In addition to varying the themes and settings of his first two
novels, Goldman introduces the schlemiel as a character in *Soldier in
the Rain*. Traditionally, the schlemiel falls below the average human
standard, but his defects are a source of delight and he is used in many
stock situations. Goldman's schlemiel, however, is not the naive
graduate of Yale but rather the teacher to whom he looks for
knowledge about women and alcohol. Even though Meltzer is the
Jew, it is Eustis who embodies the schlemiel's characteristics. This is
most clearly demonstrated when Eustis discovers his protégé's ethnic
identity and begins feeling Meltzer's head for horns. It is not the Jew
who is the schlemiel but Eustis, whose substandard behavior delights
both Meltzer and Maxwell.

Goldman's idea to have his non-Jewish hero embody the schlemiel
stereotype is a good one, but it would have been better if Meltzer's
being Jewish changed his relationship with Eustis or altered Eustis's
thoughts about Jews. If Eustis had been prejudiced against Jews and
if he found through Meltzer the fallacy of stereotypes, his discovery
that his friend was Jewish would have been significant. On the other
hand, if Meltzer's being Jewish inspired Eustis to approach other
Jews with a healthy predisposition, there would have been a sign of
growth in their relationship that would have exceeded the value of
grading women. As it is in the novel, Goldman's statement that
friendships should not be negatively altered by ethnic identity is
weakened by the fact that Meltzer and Eustis are not good friends,
and Eustis's acceptance of Meltzer's Jewishness is inconsequential.
Eustis maintains his relationship with Meltzer not because he is
liberal but because basically he does not care enough about people to
make distinctions between them.

Even though Clay, Slaughter, Meltzer, Magee, Priest, and Bobby
Jo play the institution's games, they are never rewarded for staying in
line and fostering petty injustices. Hence, they are victims and
victimizers at the same time. As the institution deadens their human
spirits, the members perpetuate the establishment's human betrayal.
In this sense, Maxwell's suicide may be paradoxically seen as one
man's attempt to negate institutional death and affirm life by taking
control of his own destiny.

On another level, Goldman affirmed the life of his book when he refused to submit to the pressure brought to bear upon him by his publishers, who insisted he change the novel's ending. "It was one of the first three books of the firm, and they said, 'We can't publish this ending. It's a downer. We guarantee you the book won't sell. Will you change it?' I said, 'I will absolutely change it, and I will give it a very happy ending, if you can guarantee me the book will sell.' They said, 'Obviously, we can't guarantee that,' and I said, 'Obviously, I can't change the ending' " (WG).

CHAPTER 5

Escaping from Reality

I   Boys and Girls Together

THE one thing I wanted to do with *Boys and Girls Together* was to write a long book. That was the creative impulse of that thing. I wanted to write a long book because I had never written one. Hiram Hayden, who was my editor for everything from *Soldier in the Rain* to, and including, *The Princess Bride*, would say, 'Just write, and we'll structure it later.' I was having a difficult time coming up with stories about the young people we were trying to balance as they went through their various lives. Anyway, I got stuck in the middle, and did some Broadway stuff, the play and the musical. I was still stuck, so I wrote *No Way to Treat a Lady*. When I finally got back to *Boys and Girls Together*, it had been a year. I said to myself, 'Am I getting in deeper trouble?' And I remember it was my brother who said, 'Well, give yourself a week or two to write it, and if you can't, stop it.' And then I wrote it in a week, I guess. I wrote very quickly, but I remember writing in tremendous pain. I have a bad back. I have a thin disc in the base of my spine that goes in and out, and a lot of it is mental and a lot of it is real. I use it. If I don't want to lift something, I say, 'Oh, my back is hurting.' That went out just when I was about to start the final section of *Boys and Girls Together*. We had the house in Princeton, and I had, at this point, seven or eight hundred pages, and I knew that I was down to the last two hundred. Those last pages were written in intense pain. They were written on sleeping pills at night so I could get to sleep and wake-up pills in the morning so I could unfog myself. The sitting was extremely uncomfortable. I remember when I finished it, I walked outside after one of those wild rushes I have—fifteen or twenty pages a day—and sat on a child's swing in my backyard and thought, 'I don't have any more stories to tell.' *The Temple of*

54

Gold was basically my childhood; *Your Turn to Curtsy, My Turn to Bow* was my camp; *Soldier in the Rain* was the army; and *Boys and Girls Together* was a summation. There was *No Way to Treat a Lady*—God knows what you make of that—but from then on, I've been dealing more with married people. Now obviously a great deal of that change has to do with the fact that *Boys and Girls Together* was not well received. I think if it had been, I might have tried to mine that particular area longer" (WG).

Goldman's observation that *Boys and Girls Together* was not well received is somewhat inaccurate. The *Los Angeles Times* referred to the book as "the novel of the year . . . Compelling, rich in its complications, intriguing in its characters, and . . . revealing of its time and place," and The *Cleveland Plain Dealer* claimed that the novel was "without question the most exciting piece of American fiction written in this decade." The *San Francisco Chronicle* said that Goldman had succeeded "in an operation at which most novelists since Thomas Wolfe have failed," and The *Chicago News* called the thirty-three-year-old novelist "a born storyteller, an extremely confident exhibitionist, . . . and a master whose book grapples vigorously with an assortment of familiar situations breathing fresh life into them all." In fact, Goldman received generally favorable reviews from all but one of the country's leading newspapers. In a sadistically unfair criticism for the *New York Times Book Review* (25 July 1964), Conrad Knickerbocker accused *Boys and Girls Together* of extending "the Californization of the novel. Finely packaged, it works in aerosol fashion. Two ounces of material, pressurized with a harmless gas, produce foam and noise when released." Knickerbocker insisted that the 696-page novel was written as a treatment for a screenplay and attacked Goldman for aspiring to join Harold Robbins, Irving Stone, Leon Uris, and Herman Wouk atop a "golden world glittering with best-seller lists, in-store promotions, paperback rights, foreign rights, movie rights, maybe even an interview with Jack Paar."

Goldman overreacted to Knickerbocker's criticism: "I'll tell you when I stopped reading reviews. *Boys and Girls Together* was three years of my life, and I thought it was not what I meant. It was depressing, and not at all what I had meant when I started. It's so hard to fill that many pages, and I thought, 'Well, it's not what I meant, but at least they'll have to think I'm serious. Nobody would write this depressing a book, in which nobody gets what they want and everybody fails, if you're trying to be Harold Robbins.' There was a review of *Boys and Girls Together* that I remember very clearly. It was one of the most painful reviews of my life by a critic from the *New York Times* called Conrad Knickerbocker. The review compared me with Harold Robbins, and I thought, 'You never read Harold Robbins. They get what they want in that world, and this is basically a cold, unpleasant book.' I remember for a month I was on the verge of tears."

Goldman recovered slightly from the blow of Knickerbocker's review after reading one by Robert Kirsch of the *Los Angeles Times* (24 June 1964). Kirsch "said terrific things about the book, but that's not the point. What he said was what I had written. He saw what I wrote. I wrote him a letter saying, 'I can't tell you what that review meant to me.' I got it months after the book was out. On *Boys and Girls Together*, I got a lot of good notices and a lot of bad notices, but most of them were misreadings. When I read Kirsch's review, I thought, 'Well, at least I didn't fail entirely.' That was the last time I ever read a review" (WG).

Kirsch correctly recognized that both the power and the flaws of *Boys and Girls Together* stem "from the personal histories of the afflicted" characters, who are unable to "understand and act on the concept of love." After criticizing Goldman's weak presentation of the protagonists' individual case studies in the first third of the novel, Kirsch calls the remainder of the novel "superb, a brilliant evocation of the sense and spirit of these lonely, brutalized, self-hating, confused people . . . And the novel, in toto, gives us a picture of that nether world, unlike any I have yet seen in fiction."

As its title implies, *Boys and Girls Together* relates the story of young people who have not reached maturity. Well beyond innocence, however, Goldman's protagonists are neurotically petty and spiritually sterile. They are unable to love either themselves or others. They are sexually inadequate, divided by guilts, alienated, aimless, bored, and rootless. They long to escape, but what is born out of desperation and hopelessness ends not in optimism or self-reliance, but in pessimism, hopelessness, confusion, and death.

The first of Goldman's escapists in *Boys and Girls Together* is Aaron Fire. Like Raymond Trevitt of *The Temple of Gold* and Eustis Clay of *Soldier in the Rain*, Aaron has the ability to rebound from defeat, but he fails ever to be born into a new man. The son of a New York lawyer and Southern aristocratic mother who live in Princeton, Aaron suffers at an early age from the death of his father. Unloved by either his mother or his older sister, Deborah,

Aaron develops an early dislike for castrating women, and, shortly after entering Princeton University, discovers his homosexuality.

After his graduation, Aaron is drafted into the army, where he meets Branch Scudder, a homosexual whose mother is a different kind of castrater than Aaron's. Whereas Charlotte rejected Aaron after the death of his father, Rose Scudder dominates her husband, Howard, and smothers her son with the sheer strength of her unbending will. When Howard is killed in action during World War II, Branch is left without a male identity-figure and learns to emulate his mother, who symbolizes those women who play on their children's fears, guilts, and inadequacies in the name of doing them good.

During his tour in the Army, Branch, who fancies himself to be a producer, initiates a friendship with Aaron, who is seriously thinking about how to begin a writing career. Aaron hates Branch's effeminacy, a sign of the homosexuality he hates in himself, but he is willing to be his friend because of the pleasures his money affords.

In charge of Branch and Aaron is Sergeant Terry, a castrating homosexual whose importance in the novel lies not so much in the sadistic orders he gives Aaron to fulfill but in the comments he offers about novel writing. In a tone of voice mildly reminiscent of Maxwell Slaughter's in *Soldier in the Rain*, Sergeant Terry tells Aaron that "writers write out of revenge" (p. 265).[1] Aaron, of course, never writes anything that is not vindictive, but, surprisingly, neither does Goldman, who says, "Vengeance is a very strong-sounding word. Retaliation might be better, but I don't believe it. Writing is an act of vengeance."

After his discharge from the Army, Aaron begins writing the novel that he imagines will bring him wealth and fame, but *Autumn Wells*, "cribbed equally from *Rebecca, The Great Gatsby,* and *Catcher in the Rye*" (p. 398), is an incredible romance that he cannot get published. Nevertheless, Aaron's reaction to David Boardman of Kingsway Press is similar to the successful Goldman's reaction to publishers in general. Aaron tells us he "had always envisioned a publishing house as being a small brownstone in an old part of town with frayed rugs on the floors and walls stuffed with books . . . Kingsway Press, where he stood, looked like a Hollywood version of an advertising agency . . . it was sterile enough to double as a hospital . . . hostile modern. And not a book in sight . . . And if Kingsway resembled an ad agency. Dave Boardman continued the image" (pp.

401–2). Talking about his own attitudes toward the publishing business, Goldman says, "Unless you've been in publishing, you don't know how dumb editors are. Dumb is the wrong word. They're basically like advertising people. They're media people, and what they've read is everything from the first year that they became editors. . . . When I say they're like admen, I mean an advertising executive, who has the Pepsi account in his pocket, jumps from agency to agency, upwardly mobile, always his weapon being, 'I've got the Pepsi account.' An editor, if he has a writer who is successful, in that same situation will jump from firm to firm. That's what publishing basically is. It was a crushing disappointment to me when I met my first editor, a young adman who hadn't read spit, but who has had a very successful career, and is one of the top editors of Doubleday, which is exactly where he should be because he can publish somebody's memoirs. That's what he's good at. He's a merchandiser. No one ever told me that."

Interestingly, Aaron's reaction to the rejection of *Autumn Wells* is identical to Goldman's after the publication of *The Temple of Gold:* "He went to museums when he felt like it, and he window-shopped when he felt like it, but mostly he went to the movies" (p. 450). What was purgatory to Goldman, Aaron enjoys, but he eventually emerges from it to accept Branch's invitation to live together and write a play that the rich friend can produce.

During the writing of *Madonna With Child,* Aaron's relationship with Branch seems to improve. Although he dislikes prostituting himself for material comforts, Aaron learns to appreciate his friend's generosity. On the other hand, Branch, who cannot bring himself to offend Aaron by telling him what he truly thinks of the play any more than he can reverse the inflationary progress reports he has given his mother about it, only pretends to be content. In an attempt to save the play with a good cast, Branch hires Rudy Miller and makes Aaron rewrite the play with the actor in the lead role.

Although Aaron and Branch do not meet him until the second half of Goldman's novel, the reader has been following Rudy's attempts to flee his parent's exploitation of him since the opening chapters of the book. Until he is six years old, Rudy is protected by the obsessive opportunism of Sid and Esther Miller by his grandfather Tuck, but when the old man dies and Sid's attempt to run an inherited delicatessen fails, Rudy's parents teach their son to sing "God Bless America" and arrange for him to audition before a movie agent. During a fight between his parents over how he should look for the audition, Rudy leaves their apartment, but instead of reporting to the agent, the boy has his head shaved by a local barber. When Rudy returns home, Sid sees what his son has done and beats him senseless.

Surviving similar but less physically damaging incidents at the hands of Sid and Esther, Rudy grows up, writes a book about his kind grandfather, and moves to New York. There he teams up with Aaron, Branch, and Jenny Divers, an aspiring young actress who is having an unhappy love affair with Charley Fiske. Walt Kirkaby, the play's director, is happily in love with a woman named Tony, who claims to be a virgin.

In the tradition of Dos Passos's *U.S.A.* and Mailer's *The Naked and the Dead*, Goldman intertwines the individual lives of Aaron, Branch, Rudy, Jenny, and Walt, as well as the lives of a large cast of characters who embody their most important influences since the time they were children. Together, they work hard on *Madonna With Child*, but can't compensate for Aaron's poorly written script.

The day of the play's opening, Branch throws a preperformance party that turns out to be anything but a celebration. At the party is Rose Scudder, who confirms her son's homosexuality, and Aaron, who gets back at Tony for saying that *Madonna With Child* was a hopelessly bad play by telling Walt that his girlfriend is not the virgin she claims to be. When Sid Miller arrives at the party to badger his son into signing papers that will commit Esther to an insane asylum and free Sid to have an affair with an influential woman in Chicago, Rudy throws himself off the apartment fire escape.

Because Rudy has no understudy, *Madonna With Child* never opens. With the exception of Aaron, who becomes the personal slave of a sadistic, but financially well-endowed playwright, Goldman's characters retreat from their initiatory experience to whatever comfort they can find in relationships with their parents or lovers.

Searching for happiness, the fulfillment of their dreams, or a purpose in life, Goldman's characters are questers as well as escapists. Rejecting both their old and newly discovered values, their flights do not lead them to maturity. Nevertheless, they do discover new identities for themselves.

How effective are the escapes offered by these new identities? Judging from the fate of Goldman's young people, death, as it is represented in the suicides of Maxwell Slaughter of *Soldier in the Rain* and Rudy Miller of *Boys and Girls Together*, is the only complete escape from life. For the rest of Goldman's protagonists, however, death is too final. It removes the possibility of a new identity; nothing can be gained by it. Even if the escapist's experience is negative, the knowledge it affords symbolizes growth and life-affirmation, the central concern of all Goldman's works.

Traditional escapists, no longer capable of adhering to beliefs they once had, run in the hope of finding something better. Jenny and Walt of *Boys and Girls Together*, Peter Bell of *Your Turn to Curtsy, My Turn to Bow*, and Eustis Clay of *Soldier in the Rain* fit this category. Jenny and Walt could have existed comfortably in their hometowns, but they move to New York in the hope of improving themselves. Walt and Peter use their daydreams to create illusions of life that are better than the realities they encounter. Eustis, like Walt, sustains his meaningless everyday life with fantasies of self-grandeur, that, of course, he is incapable of achieving.

Conversely, the escapism of Aaron, Branch, and Rudy of *Boys and Girls Together* and Raymond Trevitt of *The Temple of Gold* is an act of desperation rather than hope. Their home lives drive them to find alternative life-styles and identities in new occupations, institutions, and cities. Fleeing society's call to accept adult responsibilities, Raymond is driven from Athens to the army, school, and marriage in a series of unsuccessful attempts to protect his innocence. After his final release from the hospital, Raymond returns to Zock's grave only to depart from there on another doomed, wandering quest.

On the other hand, Aaron, who prostitutes himself for material comforts, and Branch, who returns to Ohio to live with his mother, might well say, "I been there before." For them, there is no territory that they can light out for, ahead of the rest. What territory there is, as Raymond realizes but refuses to accept, lies in the past. While the final resolutions of Aaron and Branch signify the hopelessness that is born out of desperation, Rudy's death symbolizes the ultimate reaction to the spiritual bankruptcy that is brought about when a hopeless escape turns in upon itself. In addition to demonstrating the discrepancy between what life is and what it could be, the flights of Goldman's characters manifest the dislocation of life in its transition from one generation to the next. Unlike their children, none of Goldman's parent-characters is an escapist.

Part of the reason why Mr. and Mrs. Trevitt of *The Temple of Gold* fail to understand their son's reckless behavior lies in the fact that they are too busy establishing their own identities to notice the trouble Raymond is having with his. Though not an educated man, Jacob Bell of *Your Turn to Curtsy, My Turn to Bow* has worked hard to make himself a wealthy and respected member of the Athens community, but his perseverance does not rub off on his daydreaming son. Mrs. Meltzer and Emmy, the only adults in *Soldier in the Rain*, recognize the dead life fostered by the military and rescue the innocent Jerry from the soldiers whom the army protects from civilian life. In *Boys and Girls Together*, Mrs. Firestone overcomes her husband's death and her own lack of education, married off her daughter without a scandal, and modestly supports herself while her son must rely on Sergeant Terry, Branch, and the playwright Stagpole, to provide him the material pleasures that he cannot attain by himself. When Rose's husband dies, she turns the family's faltering real estate business into a prosperous enterprise, raises Branch by herself, and pays most of the bills he runs up. Unlike their son, who heads for a fire escape every time there is a crisis, Sid and Esther Miller confront each other on whatever issues divide them. Sid fails in his attempt to run Turk's delicatessen, but he does become a successful insurance salesman. While Walt Kirkaby dreams about being a hero, his father changes his small hardware store into the largest franchise of its kind in St. Louis.

Because of a difference in the goals they set, Goldman's parents succeed while their children fail. The parents aim mostly for material things and usually achieve them through hard work, developed skills, and a little luck. With the exception of Eustis Clay in *Soldier in the Rain*, the aspirations of Goldman's young people are not quite so tangible. Protecting their innocence, rejecting the values of their guardians, and attempting to be successful writers, directors, actors, and producers, most of Goldman's protagonists reveal a desire to achieve something beyond material comfort. With the exception of Aaron and Eustis, Goldman's boys and girls are born into the good things that their parents have worked all their lives to give them. Consequently, they seek satisfaction in areas other than those provided. That the escapes of Goldman's personae are mostly self-defeating, however, does not invalidate their intensity. On the contrary, the degree of their failures only serves to further indicate the necessity that caused them.

At the end of *The Temple of Gold*, Raymond Trevitt's flight embodies something of Huck Finn's hope that some contentment can be found in geographical escape. The reader, however, knows from Raymond's trips to Crystal City, Camp Scott, and Cambridge that Goldman's first young hero can never flee that inescapable part of his being known as his past. When Eustis Clay leaves the wasteland, as it is depicted in Camp Scott, he carries with him his illusory hope of material prosperity. Seeing all their energies leading to death and betrayal, the characters of *Boys and Girls Together* conclude that there are no satisfactory alternatives. Life is hopeless. Nevertheless, suicide is not the answer; man must find a way to affirm life over death whenever his identities fail him. One way of achieving affirmation in the wasteland, Goldman seems to be saying, is through endurance.

II   No Way to Treat a Lady

"*No Way to Treat a Lady,* which is the only book of mine that was ever published under a pseudonym, and which ever got a good review from the *New York Times,* Hiram Hayden, my editor, didn't know what to do with. He didn't know, like, or read mysteries. There was a great feeling that *Boys and Girls Together* was going to establish me as a critical figure, which, of course, was the reverse of what happened, and Hiram kept saying, 'I think you'll damage yourself if you bring this out first. Why don't you try and get it published under a pseudonym?' We went to one or two houses, and it was rejected, and we went to the paperback original place, and they said, 'Sure.' It came out, and got the best reviews of anything I've ever been connected with" (WG).

Originally published under the pseudonym "Harry Longbaugh," the real name of the Sundance Kid, a gunfighter and subject of Goldman's screenplay *Butch Cassidy and the Sundance Kid* (1969), *No Way to Treat a Lady* (1964) differs significantly from anything Goldman had written previously and prefigures the main concerns of his most recent novels, *Marathon Man* (1974) and *Magic* (1976). It was republished under the name of William Goldman in 1968.

No Way to Treat a Lady narrates the experience of three murderers, all of whom react in their own way to their castrating mothers. Kit Gil, the fatherless son of a deceased actress, murders women who resemble his domineering mother. Impersonating women as well as other men, Kit cons his unsuspecting victims into inviting him into their apartments. Once inside, he strangles them, strips them of their clothing, sits them on their toilet seats, draws the imprint of a kiss on their foreheads, and telephones Morris Brummell, the detective in charge of the case, to report his murders and the disguises he uses to effect them. Morris, the son of a "Jewish Mother," is in love with Sarah Stone, a "shiksa" tenant whom he once questioned about a murder Kit had committed in her building.

Kit's pattern of deaths and reports breaks when Johnny Temple-ton, another product of overprotecting motherhood, rapes and murders the beautiful young model, Cloris St. Johns, and then tries to pin the blame on Kit by propping his victim on a toilet seat and drawing a pair of lips on her forehead. Upset that his methods have been adopted by another killer, sickened at the thought of rape, and unable to place much confidence in the ability of Morris, Kit decides to catch the "copycat" by himself. Following his suspect, Kit saves a young girl's life by attacking Templeton before he can gain entrance to her building. The two murderers create a disturbance, however, and are arrested, but the police interpret the incident as a "lovers' spat," and let them go. Shortly after their release, Kit telephones Johnny and threatens him with a surprise attack on his life. Johnny retaliates by firing a gun at Kit, who saves himself by hopping into the only vacant taxi in the area. When he returns to his house, however, Kit notices the light he left on is out and correctly surmises that Johnny is waiting for him inside.

Telephoning Morris, Kit offers to deliver the copycat, whom he falsely accuses of killing Sarah Stone, the detective's recently mur-dered girlfriend. After outwitting Johnny and relieving him of his gun, Morris takes the law into his own hands and throws a knife between the two murderers, allowing them to finish the fight they had begun earlier in the book. Kit manages to kill Johnny but not without seriously wounding himself in the process. Instead of calling an ambulance, however, the now criminally oriented Morris initiates a death watch, thereby revenging his girlfriend's death.

Responding to the literary challenge of making credible the everyday reality of contemporary American experiences, Goldman combines four traditional narrative devices in *No Way to Treat a Lady* to establish his first departure from conventional novel forms since introducing the flashforward in *Your Turn to Curtsy, My Turn to Bow* in 1958. Combining a third-person narrative with first-person diary entries, newspaper accounts, and interviews with clinical psycholo-gists, who comment on the novel's sensational events, Goldman creates a structure that reinforces his book's theme of terror-ladden multiplicity. Nevertheless, the novel does not encompass the whole of its thematic statement. Plot and theme are always present, but they are not necessarily always in focus. Consequently, Goldman can relate incidents that, though irrelevant to the novel's plot, express a more comprehensive vision of life. Whereas the plot deals with a cop trying to solve a series of murders, the novel's theme is much more ambitious. Its wider net includes references not only to the murderers' sadistic violence but to the larger social arena in which their actions take place. As the murderers play out their scenes, the reader is constantly reminded of the other patterns of reality that, existing concurrently with his own, threaten the individual law-abiding citizen's confidence in his power to effect change and control events.

Knowing ordinary people to be generally honest and humane, Kit's disguises rely primarily on his victims' good intentions. Hence charity, in *No Way to Treat a Lady*, is as self-damaging as is innocence in Goldman's earliest novels, and, like Original Ignorance, may also adversely affect others. The mothers of the three murderers all mean well, but their attempts to dominate their sons lead to overreaction on the parts of Kit, Johnny, and Morris. Kit murders women who resemble his mother, Johnny relies on his mother's protective instincts and loneliness to create an alibi for himself, and Morris tries to strangle his mother when she is unsympathetic toward his girlfriend's death.

In a vain attempt to order the chaos brought about by the murders, the daily newspapers strive to find a pattern in the events. Of course, they fail. Contemporary events may repeat themselves, but they resist being reduced to patterns. Similarly, the patterns of behavior Goldman's characters create for themselves symbolize the individual's groping for an order through which contemporary events may be related. By abandoning the actual for mental constructs, however, man has created an overstructured civilization that occasionally forces him into lawless responses. Desperate to survive a mental world that has usurped their actual one, Kit, Johnny, and Morris slip into various forms of savagery that force Goldman's readers to reformulate continually their assumptions about people and manners. Nowhere is the illogic of violence more confused with reason than when Kit tries to prevent Johnny from killing him:

> They were close together in the darkness, but separated by trees, and Kit clung close to the one nearest him and he was about to say something when Johnny said, "I'm going to kill you!"
> "You can't. Don't you see? If you do, they'll [the police] get us both."
> "I'm going to kill you."
> "But—"
> "I'm going to kill you; you're going to die."
> "Listen to me—"
> "You're going to die."

"Listen to me, are you crazy—"
"You're going to die."
He's crazy, Kit thought. *He is!* "Fool," he screamed and then he was running again, running down through the park because there was a madman after him, a lunatic was after him and you couldn't talk to a lunatic, you couldn't *reason* with a lunatic, you could only run, run" (pp. 167–68).[2]

In any "Alice in Wonderland" (p. 110) world that has replaced reason and clarity with an "Off with their heads" violence, man's only recourse is to run, but where? Geographical escape, as it is portrayed in *The Temple of Gold* and *Boys and Girls Together*, is impossible. The new identities gained in *Soldier in the Rain* and *Boys and Girls Together* are unsatisfying. The daydreams presented in *Your Turn to Curtsy, My Turn to Bow* are limiting and inhibit action, and death, as it is understood in Goldman's other works, is too final an escape. It negates any possibility of rebirth.

When Goldman looks at contemporary society in *No Way to Treat a Lady*, he discovers mankind's public and private lives to be running on separate treadmills. Behind the bland exteriors of Morris, Kit, and Johnny lurk three desperate men whose ultimate response to the process of civilized dehumanization is murder. Of the three, only Morris tries to find some sense of purpose in love, but whatever fulfillment he experiences in his relationship with Sarah ends prematurely with the brutal murder that Kit hopes to blame on Johnny. The terror of Sarah Stone, as well as that of the other victims, symbolizes our time's matter-of-fact acceptance of violence. Consequently, the book's most sympathetic character is neither a murderer nor a murder victim, but rather Mr. Kupperman, an impotent midget who confesses to Kit's crimes in a vain attempt to become a part of the world he inhabits.

The disguises used by Kit to gain the confidence of his intended victims and their resulting sense of betrayed bewilderment further symbolize the unreality of everyday life and the powerlessness of ordinary people to distinguish between what is and what seems to be. To contain these visions of violence and impotence in an age where fact and fiction are more often than not indistinguishable and to respond as well to the explosion of the ordinary by the fabulous, Goldman has turned away from the traditional novel to a surrealistic exposition of contemporary events in *No Way to Treat a Lady*.

CHAPTER 6

Imaginative Escape

I   The Thing of It Is . . .

I put on my wall various things that I want to write- I started doing that in 1960. I have the ideas for novels listed on the wall. The idea of my new novel, *Magic*, I've had for at least ten years. It seems to me there's only been one time when I've written close behind. After I had been informed I was a pornographer and left Princeton, I took a job doctoring a movie in London, and I remember my wife and I went to Rome and to Venice, and I remember saying, 'Something is happening. There's a novel inside me and it has to do with an experience we just had in London,' where our daughter lost her doll after a visit to St. Paul's, in which we didn't have a fight, but I remember what a good place it was to have a fight because everything echoed. I gave Amos McCracken my bad back so the couple would have something to fight about. Then we went to Rome, and then to Venice.

"In Venice, something happened where somebody thought we had stolen a watch, and all those things, together with my Jewishness, and I'm desperately un-Jewish, came together. If I was a more Jewish writer, I would be a lot more acceptable because then the critics could place me. That's what they love about Malamud. They can say, 'Here's Malamud in the Jewish tradition,' or 'Here's Roth in the Jewish tradition.' Well, basically, I'm not Jewish. I wasn't bar mitzvahed, I wasn't confirmed, and I only went to Sunday school for one semester. Anyway, while we were in Venice, I found the original ghetto and I couldn't believe it. There really was an original ghetto, and I went to see it, and I remember saying to Ilene, 'I've got to get back to America because I'm going to write a novel,' and within three weeks of me seeing the ghetto, the book was completed. That's the only time I've ever written close behind a situation. Every other time it took years and years and years" (WG).

66

Unlike the protagonists of *The Temple of Gold, Your Turn to Curtsy, My Turn to Bow, Soldier in the Rain,* and *Boys and Girls Together,* the McCrackens of *The Thing of It Is . . .* do not consider themselves victims of society because they cannot lead lives of innocence, but rather they feel victimized by a society that has taught them to strive for innocence. In place of characters like Raymond Trevitt, Peter Bell, Eustis Clay, and most of the protagonists of *Boys and Girls Together,* all of whom choose to be alienated, Goldman creates three family members whose isolation from each other in *The Thing of It Is . . .* and in its sequel, *Father's Day,* is a fundamental reality of everyday living.

Reflecting the shift in perspective from which Goldman views his protagonists, the books also reveal other differences from Goldman's earlier works. Instead of dealing with a number of individuals from different families, each of these two novels concerns three members of one family. Unlike the failures of his past novels, the new protagonists are conventionally successful.

In *The Thing of It Is . . .,* Amos McCracken is a thirty-year-old Broadway show composer, whose song "Francie" is internationally popular. To salvage his faltering marriage, Amos has taken his family abroad on a vacation. The novel opens in London with Amos and his wife, Lila, bickering over insignificant matters while their daughter, Jessica, attempts to stop their latest "blisterer" by telling her parents that her doll, Cuddly, wants them to stop fighting. Remembering that he had come to London to save his marriage, Amos declares a truce that lasts until the family is inside St. Paul's Cathedral. Not wishing to climb the stairs leading to the Whispering Gallery, Amos begins to feel a legitimate but convenient pain in the lower area of his back. Spurred on by Lila's calling him a sissy, however, Amos makes his way to the gallery, where he engages his wife in an acoustically amplified argument that causes their removal from the cathedral.

Bewildered by their self-abasing hateful actions and recognizing the damage they are doing to themselves and to their daughter, Amos and Lila decide to leave Jessica with a nanny and spend a few days alone in Rome. At first they are able to enjoy their time together in the holy city without making each other irritable. By the second day, however, Amos's paranoia about being taken advantage of leads them into another embarrassing confrontation. Lila complains: "Oh Amos, there's this terrible thing going on. You're just not charming any more and what am I going to do? I knew you were a nut when I married you, but you were so charming then and I loved it, the unpredictability, but I can't cope with you now. I'm tired of being the villain of the piece. . . . I'm twenty-seven years old and I'm ready for menopause. You've run me out of resources. I'm dry" (p. 20).[1]

Amos's solution to the serious issues that Lila has raised is to buy his wife the gold watch she has always wanted. Even this lame attempt at reconciliation fails, however, when the shopkeeper accuses Lila of stealing one of the watches. Embarrassed at having been caught in the act, Lila pretends to discover the missing watch under a display case, and then loses patience with her husband, who insists on buying the watch for her.

Having communicated only on levels of misunderstanding and injurious pettiness in Rome as well as in London, Amos and Lila travel to Venice, the decay of which symbolizes the couple's romantic soul. In a cafe near San Marco, Lila brings up the idea of a separation to Amos, who agrees that it "really seems like the answer for now" (p. 137). Relieved that their true feelings have finally been brought out into the open, Amos and Lila begin to communicate like people who care for one another as they talk sincerely about reaching a compromise that is fair to both them and Jessica. Their communion, however, is short-lived. Knowing the McCrackens to be without their daughter and suspecting marital difficulties, Lila's mother flies to London, picks up Jessica, and travels on with her to Venice, where they surprise the disconcerted parents.

In retaliation against her mother, Lila takes her and Amos to visit Venice's Jewish ghetto, where her husband announces his Jewish heritage, a secret he has kept since his college days at Princeton. The offended women abandon Amos, who wallows in self-pity until a ghetto resident asks him to maintain the neighborhood's good reputation by going someplace else. Returning to his hotel, Amos's thoughts echo a theme present in all of Goldman's works: "The easiest thing . . . was to think that everything was wonderful. The second easiest thing was to think everything was shit. The third thing, the hard thing, the only hard and right and proper thing to think was this: to affirm in spite of . . ." (p. 157).

That flight is a form of affirmation seems to be symbolized by Amos's decision to leave Lila immediately and return to his work in New York. Before he can leave the hotel room, however, Lila tells Amos that she had actually tried to steal the watch he had wanted to buy her in Rome. Hearing his wife's admission of human imperfection, Amos chooses to stay with her and "affirm in spite of."

Amos's decision to choose alienation within his relationship with Lila rather than isolation outside of it marks Goldman's change of view toward the characters he has created. In his earliest novels, Goldman imitated writers such as Salinger and Fitzgerald, who saw alienation from corrupt society as a life-affirming heroic action. Goldman developed this theme to its ultimate conclusion in *Soldier in the Rain* and *Boys and Girls Together*. Of all the protagonists in Goldman's first four novels, only Aaron Fire, who prostitutes himself for material goods, Turk, who is wise to the ways of the world, and Rudy's opportunistic parents concern themselves with events that are not primarily designed to protect their innocence. Alienation in *The Thing of It Is . . .* , then, is no longer the chosen ideal of sensitive men and women but rather a fundamental reality of everyday life. Whereas *No Way to Treat a Lady* dramatically rejects the perspective of the alienated individual who withdraws from the society that has failed him by having its protagonists react to their isolation through rape and murder, *The Thing of It Is . . .* asserts the individual estrangement of its characters by emphasizing their dependence on one another.

Goldman's newly revealed ability to understate rather than dramatically display his material enables him to relate his story of the McCrackens in a novel of considerably more interest and psychological substance than his mammoth work, *Boys and Girls Together*. Rather than detail the case histories of his characters, as he did in *The Temple of Gold* and *Boys and Girls Together*, Goldman emphasizes the psychological depths and weaknesses within each individual through their everyday conversation and flashback thoughts. Through these intimate personal revelations of the McCracken family, then, Goldman asserts the universality of alienation.

The alienated individuals of *The Thing of It Is . . .* are like those of Goldman's former novels, however, in that they are destructive. Whereas the injury wrought by Goldman's earlier·protagonists resulted from their innocence, the psychological damage inflicted by Amos and Lila stems from their ideas about what constitutes maturity. Hence, society, according to Goldman, is not a complex and corrupt entity that is bent on destroying the autonomy of the individual, but rather a wicked environment in which individuals learn the philosophy of selfish alienation, that is, how to be autonomous and innocent, and therefore self-centered and destructive.

In seeming contrast to Amos and Lila stands their daughter, Jessica, who often displays the maturity that her parents lack. Even Jessica, though, learns the lesson of isolation. When she loses her doll, for example, Amos and Lila use the incident to attack each other for not caring about their daughter and compete for her affection. When Jessica's parents want to overcome their alienation from each other, they isolate themselves from their daughter by leaving her with a nanny in London while they fly to Rome.

The alienation existing among the McCracken family members stems from a deeper isolation within each individual. To vindicate the embarrassment suffered by her father, who did not have enough money to pay for a watch she had wanted as a child, Lila puts herself and Amos in an awkward position by trying to steal a watch they can well afford to purchase. Amos, on the other hand, embarrasses Lila and upsets her mother with his rude revelation that he is half-Jewish. In fact, Amos's "Kiss my Jewish ass" (p. 151) sounds very much like Eustis's blasphemous address to God at the conclusion of *Soldier in the Rain*.

Goldman's treatment of Jews is an interesting but confusing issue. In *Soldier in the Rain*, Goldman has his non-Jewish hero, Eustis Clay, embody schlemiel characteristics in order to negate the accuracy of stereotypes as they pertain to individuals. In what seems to be a reversal of this position, Goldman creates a Jewish mother-figure in *No Way to Treat a Lady* who has no characteristics other than those of the unattractive stereotype she embodies. Although being Jewish alienates Jerry Meltzer of *Soldier in the Rain* from Priest and Lenehan, he does not resent his heritage as Amos McCracken does: "And he was a Jew. Half a Jew, actually, his mother being the one cursed. 'Cursed' was really much too strong a word. Amos wasn't anti-Semitic. He just didn't care about it one way or the other, and as long as his secret was safe, he slept sound. . . . No one knew. Not his wife, not his child, not his anti-Semite mother-in-law, . . ." (p. 12). Amos says that he does not care about being Jewish, yet his secretiveness, plus his offensive climactic outburst in the ghetto, reveals that he, in fact, cares very much about it. Goldman's position in regard to his heritage may be similar. He says that he is "desperately un-Jewish," yet his preoccupation with the subject and the sometimes confused references he makes to Christianity in his fiction (see below) indicate that his Jewishness may possibly play a greater role in his novels than he is aware.

When Amos arrives at St. Paul's Cathedral, his jocular attitude, "I just hope the food's all it's cracked up to be" (p. 26), is immediately reversed by the magnificence of Wren's monument: "St. Paul's ambushed him and as he stood in the cool, quiet air he said, to his own surprise, 'Aw.' " Amos's awe as a non-Christian, un-Jewish agnostic increases with his seeing "a perfectly horrid picture by someone named Hunt and he was about to move on when he noticed the inscription underneath: *Behold I stand at the door and knock. If any man hear my voice, and open the door, I will come into him and will sup with him and he with me*" (p. 28).

Amos, like Goldman, is an outsider looking in at Christianity. What they see puzzles them. When Amos returns to St. Paul's to look for Jessica's lost doll, he again contemplates the image created by the inscription beneath Hunt's painting. Not until the end of the book does the reader discover Amos's identification with the outsider coming in when invited. When Lila admits that she was trying to steal the watch, Amos interprets her confession as her "standing at the door and knocking." Opening the door, he, thinking of the inscription, comes "into her, erect and joyous, their imperfect bodies rocking together, touching, he hoped at least temporarily, . . ." (p. 163).

The reader's confusion in *The Thing of It Is . . .* does not arise in Amos's sexual resolution, but rather in the image of one Jesus surrogate (Amos) opening the door and coming into another Jesus surrogate (Lila), who stood and knocked. On the other hand, the McCrackens' temporary union may be Goldman's improvement on Hunt's quote from Revelations 3:20. We are all Jesuses, Goldman seems to be saying, waiting for the opportunity to respond to the doors opened by other Jesuses.

If the latter is true, Amos's reunion with Lila at the end of *The Thing of It Is . . .* marks Goldman's final resolution of an issue with which he has confusedly wrestled since his first novel. In *The Temple of Gold*, Raymond compares his communion with Zock to a Catholic attending confession, and Mr. Trevitt tells his son that he is like the Christ whose father failed him in the Garden of Gethsemane. Goldman's preoccupation with images of forsaken

Christ figures becomes a crucifixion complex in *Your Turn to Curtsy, My Turn to Bow* when Chad Kimberly nails himself to a cross. In *Soldier in the Rain*, Christianity mixes with Judaism as the non-Jewish schlemiel, Eustis Clay, blasphemes his God in heaven. *Boys and Girls Together* and *No Way to Treat a Lady* present a parade of Jews who run the gamut from the gentle grandfather, Turk, to the almost inhumane mother, Mrs. Brummell. In *The Thing of It Is . . .*, Amos keeps his Jewish heritage a secret, but after purging himself of the "curse" in Venice's Jewish ghetto, he feels free to inform everyone, including elevator men in *Father's Day*, of his being half-Jewish. Amos's Christian reference, while making love to his non-Jewish wife, then, possibly announces Goldman's conclusion that people are more important than any religious heritage.

The least effective and most unimaginative of Goldman's escapists, Amos and Lila McCracken fail to improve upon their situation regardless of where they run. In the end, they fall into the security of each other's arms in the hope that whatever joy they share will not be temporary. In an age where people are alienated within themselves as well as from each other, however, the chances for a permanent positive relationship, as *The Thing of It Is . . .* and its sequel, *Father's Day*, demonstrate, are practically nil.

II   Butch Cassidy and the Sundance Kid

After the publication of *The Thing of It Is . . .*, Goldman wrote *The Season: A Candid Look at Broadway* (1969), a partially vindictive response to his experiences with the plays *Blood, Sweat, and Stanley Poole* (1961) and *Family Affair* (1962), but also a relatively accurate appraisal of the Broadway theater season of 1968. During that time, Goldman also wrote his universally popular *Butch Cassidy and the Sundance Kid*, for which he won an Academy Award for the Best Original Screenplay of 1969.

Perhaps the most accomplished storyteller in contemporary American cinema, Goldman approaches his scripts pragmatically: "I'm a novelist who happens to write screenplays. I write them to read, to catch someone's attention. Pace and narrative are much more important to me than camera setups. For me, screenplay writing is like a two-man relay race. The first man is the screenwriter, and he chugs out an idea on paper. Then comes the second man, the director. The writer hands off the script and the director takes it over the finish line."

Rarely, however, does the director cross the film's finish line with the script in the same condition in which Goldman gave it to him. Comments Goldman: "Only twice has Hollywood shot the screenplay I wrote. Once was *Harper* and once was *Butch Cassidy and the Sundance Kid*." One way for a writer to protect his script is to direct its transition to film, but Goldman does not "want to be a director or a producer. It's a strange position. I don't want power. I don't use the little power I have. I have whatever power I need in my novels in terms of being in control, and, as a general rule, screenwriting is not something about which I care a great deal."

Butch Cassidy and the Sundance Kid takes place when the American West is on the brink of civilization. Capitalists are already exploiting the country's natural resources and building railroads to carry their wealth to Eastern banks, but the new trains are easy prey to roaming bands of outlaws. Thanks to several mostly fictitious newspaper stories, the most popular band of railroad bandits is a group of petty thieves and cutthroats known as the Hole-in-the-Wall Gang. Led by George Leroy Parker, known as Butch Cassidy, and Harry Longbaugh, the Sundance Kid, the train robbers effect a series of imaginative holdups and escapes that gain for them not only money but an awesome reputation: their names are known "back East."

For one robbery attempt, however, the authorities are prepared. From a boxcar on a special train, a mounted "superposse," led by the famous lawman, Joe Lefors, emerges and begins a pursuit of Butch and Sundance that lasts for several days and seems to cover hundreds of miles. The two villains try every trick in their book of escapes but fail to elude the lawmen until they manage to leap from a dangerously high cliff into a rapidly moving river.

With train robbery quickly becoming a hazardous occupation, Butch (played by Paul Newman) and Sundance (Robert Redford) along with Sundance's girlfriend, Etta Place (Katherine Ross) decide to light out for the new territory being settled in South America. There, the bandits learn enough Spanish to ply their trade with banks: "Manos arriba. Esta es un robo" (p. 122).[2]

One day, after a successful payroll heist, Butch and Sundance ride into a small town where they are discovered by the local police, who, with the assistance of a regiment of Bolivian soldiers, open fire on the outlaw pair. Seriously wounded, the two delinquents retreat to a hut where they prepare for a last stand:

Butch and Sundance, crouched close together by a window, peering out
toward the setting sun.
Butch: I got a great idea where we should go next.
Sundance: Well I don't wanna hear it.
Butch: You'll change your mind once I tell you—
Sundance: Shut up.
Butch: O.k.; o.k.
Sundance: It was your great ideas got us here.
Butch: Forget about it . . .
Sundance: I never want to hear another of your great ideas, all right?
Butch: All right.
Sundance: Good.
Butch: Australia. . . . I figured secretly you wanted to know so I told you:
Australia.
Sundance: That's your great idea?
Butch: The latest in a long line.
Sundance (Exploding with everything he has left): Australia's no better than
here!
Butch: That's all you know.
Sundance: Name me one thing.
Butch: They speak English in Australia.
Sundance: They do?
Butch: That's right, smart guy, so we wouldn't be foreigners. And they ride
horses. And they got thousands of miles to hide out in—and a good climate,
nice beaches, you could learn to swim—
. . . Sundance: . . . I'll think about it.
Butch: Now after we—(And suddenly he stops)—wait a minute—
Sundance: What?
Butch: You didn't see Lefors out there?
Sundance: Lefors? No.
Butch: Good. For a minute I thought we were in trouble. (181–83)

I quote this passage at length because Goldman considers it an
example of his writing at its best: "The last scene in *Butch Cassidy* is a
good piece of writing. It's as good as I can do. It's based on the
premise that two men are dying, and they refuse to talk about it. If
you can give me that premise, that's a well-structured scene. I can't
do any better than that. I suppose I still know it by heart. It seems to
still flow in my mind."

Contrary to what a plot synopsis may imply, the predominant tone
of *Butch Cassidy and the Sundance Kid* is comic. When Goldman
introduces Etta Place into his story, she is seen disrobing in front of a
pistol barrel pointed at her by Sundance. As he approaches her with a
menacing expression on his face, she quips, "I wish just once you'd

get here on time." (p. 50) Unprepared for Etta's statement, the audience laughs with relief and is pleased to discover that Butch and Sundance are not dangerous desperadoes but loveable rogues.

Incorporated with this and other examples of good clean fun is Goldman's use of social stereotypes. Etta Place, not soon to be a model for Women's Liberation advocates, says, "I'm twenty-six, single, and a schoolteacher and that's the bottom of the pit" (p. 115). Sundance is appropriately macho:" . . . if you want to come with us, I won't stop you, but the minute you start to whine or make a nuisance, I don't care where we are, I'm dumping you flat", and Butch keeps things from becoming too serious: "Don't sugarcoat it like that, Sundance—tell her straight" (p. 114).

The characters in the film that are employed by "the establishment" are pictured as ineffectual and are used primarily as foils for the outlaws' wit. In addition to the bumbling sheriff, who can succeed only in making himself look foolish in front of his apathetic constituents, there is the railroad agent who resists the Hole-in-the-Wall Gang's attempt to enter his boxcar on the ground that "Mr. E. H. Harriman himself of the Union Pacific Railroad gimme this job and I never had such responsibility before and since he entrusted me to get the money through, I got to do my best, don't you see?" (p. 34). When Butch blows the agent up along with the boxcar, he tells him, "Whatever Harriman's paying you, it's not enough" (p. 36).

The comic tone of Goldman's screenplay is heightened by his romantic portrayal of the bandit-heroes. Witty, high-spirited, and fun-loving, the outlaw pair exchange one-liners with the polish of a veteran vaudeville team. Unfortunately for the viewer, their actions are one-dimensionally motivated and lack a historical perspective. Before their heroic deaths, Butch and Sundance knock off Bolivian soldiers as if they were ducks in a shooting gallery, and the victims, eager to contribute to the film's Hollywood style, fall off rooftops and the like as if they were Olympic divers. Historically, the demise of the two outlaws was not quite so romantic. After shooting three soldiers, the Sundance Kid was fatally wounded, and Butch Cassidy, fearing his eventual capture, shot himself.

III   Father's Day

Combining his practical knowledge of the Broadway theater with the sharp crisp dialogue that had become his trademark well before *Butch Cassidy and the Sundance Kid* (1969), Goldman wrote a sequel

to *The Thing of It Is . . .* and called it *Father's Day*. Like the former
novel, *Father's Day* is based on an incident that occurred in
Goldman's life.

"The producers of a play a few years back realized that the writing
of the play wasn't going well, so they fired the original writer and
brought in me and my brother because they had read a play that we
had written. Now, when you're replaced, it's very wounding, but it
happens to everybody, and you leave, but the writer we replaced
wouldn't. So that, basically, was where being fired out of town in the
novel came from, but in this case, it was terrifying because the
original writer just wouldn't leave. And I understand how terrible it
must be. The McCracken situation came from that one. The characters in the book are repeating the same group that's had an earlier hit
in the novel. The impossible way that writer acted out of a sense of
distraughtness is Amos" (WG).

Amos McCracken opens the second book of Goldman's planned
trilogy by fighting with his now divorced wife, Lila, over his
forgetting his daughter Jessica's invitation to attend her school's
visiting day for fathers. The subsequent loss of his mistress, Betsy
Epstein, on the ground that he is too involved with his family, marks
another in a series of disasters that begins with Amos's "going dry"
and consequently being fired from his most recent Broadway musical, *Annie's Day*. Unlike Goldman, who "unsticks" himself from one
work by writing another, Amos becomes anxiety-ridden and unable
to concentrate on anything but his frustrations.

After meeting with Jessica's teacher, who tells him that his
daughter has become increasingly "weary and tense" since her
parents' separation, Amos takes his six-year-old to Nathan's for a hot
dog. While there, he offers to treat her to the matinee of her choice.
When Jessica asks to see *Annie's Day*, a bitter Amos reduces the child
to tears and instead takes her to Central Park. At a playground in the
Park, the father and daughter begin playing on a set of swings until
Amos, on the verge of mentally creating a tune that will end his "dry
spell," collides with Jessica, whom he does not realize is playing near
his swing, and opens a cut on her face that requires stitches.

After rushing his daughter to a nearby hospital, reluctantly placing
her in the hands of a Puerto Rican doctor, telephoning Lila, and
listening to her threat to keep Jessica away from him, the pressures of
Amos's guilt-ridden failures begin to rapidly take their toll. Fighting a
breakdown, Amos begins creating fantasies that he soon cannot
distinguish from reality. Overcoming imaginary dogs, policemen,

and bullet wounds, Amos takes Jessica to La Guardia Airport, where he buys two tickets to Miami. The two are prevented from escaping, however, by Jessica, who, sensing the value of imagination in grasping reality, asks her father to get Pierre.

Pierre, an earlier invention of Amos's imagination and as real to Jessica as her parents, first appeared at the McCracken home shortly after Amos was fired from *Annie's Day*. Irritated by his mental block, Amos was spending a great deal of time sulking around the house trying to find issues over which he and Lila could fight. Caught in the middle was Jessica, who, among other things, lost her appetite. To get his daughter to eat the meals her mother prepared for her, Amos disguises himself as the famous French chef, Pierre, who would cook for Jessica only when he heard that the market was selling enough food to feed three members of the McCracken family instead of two. Consequently, Jessica's appetite improved as she and Pierre became friends. When Pierre appears at the airport, Jessica asks him to take her home. Disappointed, yet understanding the needs of his daughter, whom he loves, Amos returns Jessica to her mother.

The alienation that divided each of the McCracken family members within him or herself and isolated each from the others as well increases in *Father's Day*. Amos and Lila are divorced and no longer concerned with saving their relationship. Whereas Jessica was once one of the several important interests they shared, she is now their only connecting link. When he lived at home, Amos enjoyed a singularly close relationship with Jessica. Now, however, he relies on his creation, Pierre, to establish the communion he has lost. Interestingly, the alienation separating Amos from his wife, mistress, and daughter does not stem from a loss of love. In the cases of Lila and Betsy, there is not much love with which to begin. Betsy seems to genuinely care for Amos, as Lila once did, but her feelings are not reciprocated. Nevertheless, Amos displays an inordinate amount of affection for Jessica. In fact, he loves her in an extraordinary way—he actually listens to her, devotes himself wholeheartedly to acting out characters for her pleasure, and plans elaborate schemes to delight her. Unfortunately, Amos's professional interests intrude on whatever happiness they might share, and their love for each other becomes reduced to communication through Pierre.

Kit Gil's violent response to the absurd world he inhabits in *No Way to Treat a Lady* prefigures Amos's desperate appeal to his imagination in *Father's Day*. Like *No Way to Treat a Lady*, which is told through a third-person narrator, Brummell's first-person diary, and daily newspaper accounts, *Father's Day* is narrated on three different levels of communication: action, remembrance, and fantasy. Unlike *No Way to Treat a Lady*, however, the three levels of *Father's Day* are often indistinguishable from one another. The introductory clause of Goldman's first sentence refers to Betsy, his mistress, yet the rest of the sentence and the ensuing eleven pages lead the reader to believe that Amos is talking about Lila. Not until Lila telephones Amos to remind him of his "Father's Day" commitment (p. 18)[3] does the reader realize that Goldman's songwriter is with someone other than his wife. This blending of characters almost to the point of their being indistinguishable foreshadows the desperate fantasies that neither Amos nor the reader can readily distinguish from reality.

On his return from the hospital after telephoning Lila about Jessica's accident, Amos imagines that a German shepherd attacks him. At first, Amos runs, but later, when he notices the unprotected Dr. Contreras coming toward him with Jessica in her arms, he turns and fights the beast. Having killed the imaginary dog, Amos credits himself with being a hero. Similarly, when Amos imagines that Lila has reported his having kidnapped their daughter, he also imagines that a policeman, who recognizes him as a famous Broadway musical composer, wants Jessica's father for questioning. Making "the jump to fantasy with no sweat" (p. 194), Amos runs throughout the Times Square area in a desperate attempt to lose "Chubbycheeks." Failing to elude this second threat to his and Jessica's happiness, Amos, as he did with the mad dog, turns to fight. The desperate father hits his pursuer with a rock, but fails to reach the safety of Betsy's building before being shot. Once inside Betsy's apartment, the reader discovers that Amos has not been wounded by a policeman's bullet, yet his desperate fantasies are so vividly described that they surrealistically surpass the actual violence of the murders in *No Way to Treat a Lady*.

An important part of the McCrackens' isolation from each other stems from the pressures placed on Amos to succeed. Once he has become a successful songwriter, Amos notices that his work has separated him from everyone but his daughter. Nevertheless, incidents such as Lila's confession about stealing the watch prove that Amos and his wife can still attain an occasional positive contact. When Amos is fired from *Annie's Day*, however, he can only fight with Lila and has to invent Pierre, his imaginative construct, to communicate with Jessica.

Unlike Kit Gil and Morris Brummell of *No Way to Treat a Lady*, who suffer tremendous pressure to make themselves into something of which their mothers can approve, Amos struggles to avoid the failures his mother-in-law predicts for him and her daughter. Whether striving to succeed or avoid failure, however, the protagonists of Goldman's three novels find themselves alienated from human affection. Consequently, Kit and Morris are able to become murderers while Amos draws on a larger psychoanalytic arsenal to attack his intellectually inferior wife.

While undergoing analysis with Dr. Marx, Amos learns to affirm in spite of the pressure. Unfortunately, Amos asserts his strength by cruelly analyzing the faults of others. An eventual victim of his own victimizing, Amos finds he is isolated from himself as well as from Lila and Jessica. Together, the McCracken family members symbolize a genuine study in alienation, that is, of people who are as firmly attached to one another as they are hostile to one another, and whose hostility rises out of the conditions of their attachment.

Gradually beaten by his domestic failures, romantic desertion, and professional pressure, Amos tries to give substance to his life by inventing fantasies and incorporating them with everyday reality. As Goldman presents them, the fantasies are real, to the reader as well as to Amos. Imperceptibly, the fantasies become indistinguishable until the vision clears and the reader can say, "Oh yes, that was real, and that was not." In this novel, as in real life, there are no signposts to mark the way.

Ironically, one of Amos's fantasies returns him to the reality of his daughter's needs. Aware that something is wrong with her father, Jessica asks Pierre to return her to her mother, and Amos obliges. The adept blending of almost indistinguishable fantasy and reality with Amos's paranoia, hostility, and guilt for his failures as a husband, father, lover, and songwriter marks *Father's Day* as one of Goldman's best books and solidifies his maturity as a writer.

Adds Goldman: "*Father's Day* is book two of a trilogy. I may never write the third book, which is called *The Settle for Less Club*. It was going to be Amos in Hollywood when the movie is being made, and the same people are getting together. What happens is, Amos decides to marry the girl, who was his mistress, and wants to bring the daughter out for the wedding, but his ex-wife comes too. The two of them get together, and what you do in life, basically, is settle for less.

"Anyway, I don't know if I'll ever write it because the movie business has shifted. At the time I was writing the trilogy, it was standard that if the musical was a hit on Broadway, they would make a movie out of it, but that doesn't happen anymore. The first one to be brought out in years has been *Chorus Line*. Most of them failed, and they were expensive to do. So I was going to write two Hollywood novels, and that was one of them, and I've been carrying that book around in my head, but it's no problem to write Amos because I know how he thinks."

CHAPTER 7

Fantastic Escape: The Princess Bride

I loved writing *The Princess Bride;* it's the only thing I've ever written that I really care about. I remember I was wildly close to my subconscious. It was the closest I've been to anything I've written since *The Temple of Gold.* I just let whatever happened happen. It's the only thing I've ever written that I think is good.

"The book is an abridgement of a book that doesn't exist. I didn't start with that idea. The first thing I wrote was the section that is now in the book called 'Chapter One, The Bride,' which is fifteen or twenty pages long, and the second thing I wrote was the chapter, 'The Groom,' which is three or four pages long, and then I was dry. I had all these things, and I was desperate to get them out because I didn't want to write all the crap that I didn't know how to do.

"I had a fencing scene, and a fighting scene, and a scene with a giant snake, and a scene with a monstrous this and a monstrous that, and I didn't know how to connect them. Then, suddenly, I got the idea of what if it's an abridgement?

"The frame of the book was not meant to be a literary trick. The opening chapter about a Goldman, who is doing work in Los Angeles on *The Stepford Wives,* is to give a reality to Morgenstern, to the book that I'm abridging. Once I got the idea that it was all an abridgement, and I could legitimately go from good part to good part, it opened up on me like nothing I've ever done has opened up on me. I was writing! I didn't know what it was, but I knew that I was running very close to my subconscious, and I didn't know that it was so terribly important to me. I guess it's probably the most important thing I've ever written or ever will write. I don't know why. I don't even want to think about why.

"It began as a children's book. I still have the opening chapters somewhere. The name Buttercup is from Gilbert and Sullivan. Humperdinck seemed to me a gooney name, and it seemed to go along with Buttercup. Florin, Guilder stem from when the book was a children's book. As I gradually became obsessed with it, the names changed. Inigo is a legitimate name and so is Westley. The book darkens and stops being childlike, and gets into all sorts of things.

"I've gotten more responses on *The Princess Bride* than on everything else I've done put together—all kinds of strange outpouring letters. Something in *The Princess Bride* affects people. So many letters think it really was a book.

"Usually I have a family picture on the back of my books. I was careful on this book not to have a picture of my family because I claim I have a wife who's a shrink and a fat son. At one time, I was toying with the idea of getting a skinny lady and fat boy to pose with me for a picture, but I was not interested in doing a trick. So many people have talked about that and about Morgenstern as if he really existed. Some people would remember it from their childhood, and some people will talk about what a wonderful thing I did abridging this book. I'm always amazed at that, as an author, because what would I have done had the book really existed? Abridging a book is nothing. *Reader's Digest* does it every month.

"Some of *The Princess Bride* is really good storytelling. When the man in black is after the three villains is really good. The fencing scene is a really good scene. I'm really proud of that. There's not a lot in my life that I have to be proud of, but there's a great deal in that book that I'm genuinely moved by.

"The one time in my life that I've been moved by my writing, when I was writing, was the scene where Westley dies. It's when the father skips and the kid says, 'No, no, you skipped something,' and the father says, 'You're taking this awful seriously,' and the kid says, 'I'll find the book whatever so tell me what happens.' And the father says, 'Westley dies,' and the kid asks, 'Westley dies?' Then the father has to tell him that Prince Humperdinck killed him, and then the father closes the book and has to go away, and the boy starts to cry, and I began to cry also, just like the boy, because what I said about him I felt for myself also" (WG).

In an undated letter to Hiram Hayden, to whom *The Princess Bride* is dedicated, Goldman explains the genesis and meaning of the best book he has written to date:

I thought the best way to give some notions on the book was to set down as quickly as I could the way the book came to happen.

I remember putting, in despair and desperation, a piece of paper on the wall in front of my desk (I tape things on the walls on occasion) and it said, '*I must write something soon.'* I had been writing, as you know, a lot, steadily, but always movie adaptations. Then I had a dreadful fight with my director, which was painful for us both and this was after I had finished the first draft of a movie. In my contract, they had 90 days (they being the movie studio) to decide on whether or not to go on with re-writing and I found myself, quite surprisingly, trapped. I couldn't take on another film job; I couldn't do anything but just sit there and wait. Then the notion came to me: jerk, write something of your own.

I had asked my daughters, Jenny and Susanna, years ago, what they wanted me to write them a book about and one of them said "princesses" and the other said "brides" and I said, 'Okay, that'll be the title, THE PRINCESS BRIDE.' (I had even tried starting it a couple of years ago, when I was trapped in Hollywood, and I did about two pages, starting with where Buttercup is introduced to the mob, which is now I guess the start of chapter four or five. Anyway, that's why the names of the early people are kids' names, Humperdinck and Buttercup.)

Anyway, I wrote the first chapter which basically could be subtitled 'How Buttercup became the most beautiful girl in the world.' It ran maybe 20 pages. Then I wrote chapter two, 'The Groom,' in which I introduced this horrible fellow who was to be the groom. That ran maybe four pages. And then I was dry, I had no more to write. I was totally and completely dead.

Then, thank God, I got the notion of the abridgement. And when that idea hit, everything changed. Tennessee Williams says there are three or four days when you are writing a play that the piece opens itself to you, and the good parts of the play are all from those days. Well, THE PRINCESS BRIDE opened itself to me. I never had a writing experience like it. I went back and wrote the chapter about Bill Goldman being at the Beverly Hills Hotel and it all just came out. I never felt as strongly connected emotionally to any writing of mine in my life. It was totally new and satisfying and it came as such a contrast to the work I had been doing in the films that I wanted to be a novelist again.

Somehow what the book is (beyond being a classic tale of true love and high adventure) and what the book is about (besides the fact that life isn't fair) is all tied up in the little part in the chapter when the 'me' character has pneumonia and his father starts reading and the kid says, has it got any sports in it? And the father says—Fencing * Fighting* Torture * True Love * Hate* Revenge * Giants * Hungers * Bad Men * Good Men * Beautiful Women * Snakes * Spiders * Beasts of all natures and descriptions * Pain * Death * Brave Men * Cowards * Strong Men * Chases * Escapes * Captures * Lies * Truths * Passions * Miracles *
And then the kid says, 'Sounds okay, I'll try to stay awake.'

Then later, when it turns out 'my' kid hasn't read it he says, 'I didn't like it, Daddy,' And I think: How could you not like it? Passions. Truths. Miracles. Giants. True Love.

And I guess, arrogantly enough, Hiram, *mon vieux*, that's how I feel. How can anyone not like a book with giants and truths and passions and true love and miracles?

The book means a great deal to me. Most of us are clever enough at dissembling to hide our real loves and neuroses behind some guise or other. I don't know what THE PRINCESS BRIDE says about me but I bet it's plenty. I'm in there somewhere, wouldn't you say?

Anyway, burn this letter and I'll talk to you next week.[1]

   Goldman's idea of writing an "abridgement" to a "classic" is his most ambitious and most successful sleight-of-hand trick. Charmingly done, his literary loax leaves the reader with none of the hostile reactions felt toward such early narrative tricks as Raymond's marrying Terry Clark in *The Temple of Gold*.
   To give the fictitious author "S. Morgenstern" and his *Classic Tale of True Love and High Adventure* a sense of authenticity, Goldman precedes his "abridgement" with an amusing introduction that fictionalizes some actual incidents in his life. While working on *The Stepford Wives* in Hollywood, the Goldman of the novel remembers his "father" reading "Morgenstern's" *The Princess Bride* to him when he was a child suffering from pneumonia and the effect the book had on his life. Not only did *The Princess Bride* change the fictionalized Goldman from a sports freak to a lover of adventure novels, but it nurtured in his imagination scenes that he claims to have later incorporated into such important works as *Butch Cassidy and the Sundance Kid*.
   Upset with his "son" for not liking *The Princess Bride*, the fictitious Goldman flips through some of the book's pages until he realizes that "Morgenstern wasn't writing any children's book; he was writing a kind of satiric history of his country and the decline of the monarchy in Western civilization. But my father only read me the action stuff" (p. 13).[2] Reading for the first time his "favorite book in all the world" (p. 3), "Goldman" decides to write a "good parts" version like the one his father told him. All "abridging remarks and other comments" (p. 41) are in red type.

Goldman's "abridgement" begins with Buttercup, a beautiful dairymaid, who is taken from her home and true love, Westley, to be Prince Humperdinck's bride. Shortly after Prince Humperdinck announces his bethrothal to Buttercup, the young princess, by this time a three-year graduate of Royalty School, is kidnapped by three desperadoes who have been hired to murder her in such a way that the kingdom of Guilder will be held responsible for her death, thereby giving the prince and his chief advisor, Count Rugen, the excuse they need to attack Florin's weaker neighbor.

Sailing the Florin Channel to Guilder, the kidnappers notice that they are being pursued by a man in black. At the Cliffs of Insanity, Vizzini, the leader of the murderers, orders Inigo to wait for the man following them and destroy him. The son of Domigo Montoya, the best swordsmith in all of Europe, Inigo fell into the life of crime after his ten-year search to find the six-fingered man who murdered his father had failed. A wizard swordsman, which is one step above a master, Inigo decides to make his upcoming duel interesting by keeping his sword in his left hand. In what may well be the most exciting sword fight ever narrated, Inigo and the man in black battle above the Cliffs of Insanity. I cite the entire sword fight passage not only to give the flavor of Goldman's style, but also to suggest something about Goldman's estimate of his own narrative gift. For Goldman has remarked: "Some of *The Princess Bride* is really good storytelling. When the man in black is after the three villains is really good. The fencing scene is a really good scene. I'm really proud of that. There's not a lot in my life that I have to be proud of, but there's a great deal in that book that I'm genuinely moved by."

The man in black kept advancing, and Inigo was aware that behind him now he was coming closer and closer to the edge of the Cliffs, but that could not have concerned him less. The important thing was to outthink the enemy, find his weakness, let him have his moment of exultation.

Suddenly, as the Cliffs came ever nearer, Inigo realized the fault in the attack that was flashing at him: a simple Thibault maneuver would destroy it entirely, but he didn't want to give it away so soon. Let the other man have the triumph a moment longer; life allowed so few.

The Cliffs were very close behind him now.

Inigo continued to retreat; the man in black continued advancing.

Then Inigo countered with the Thibault.

And the man in black blocked it.

He blocked it!

Inigo repeated the Thibault move and again it didn't work. He switched to Capo Ferro, he tried Bonetti, he went to Fabris; in desperation he began a move used only twice, by Sainct.

Nothing worked!

The man in black kept attacking.

And the Cliffs were almost there.

Inigo never panicked—never came close. But he decided some things very quickly, because there was no time for long consultations, and what he decided was although the man in black was slow in reacting to moves behind trees, and not much good at all amidst boulders, when movement was restricted, yet out in the open, where there was space, he was a terror. "You are most excellent," he said. His rear foot was at the cliff edge. He could retreat no more.

"Thank you," the man in black replied. "I have worked very hard to become so."

"You are better than I am," Inigo admitted.

"So it seems. But if that is true, then why are you smiling?"

"Because," Inigo answered, "I know something you don't know."

"And what is that?" asked the man in black.

"I'm not left-handed," Inigo replied, and with those words, he all but threw the six-fingered sword into his right hand, and the tide of battle turned.

The man in black retreated before the slashing of the great sword. He tried to side-step, tried to parry, tried to somehow escape the doom that was now inevitable. But there was no way. He could block fifty thrusts; the fifty-first flicked through, and now his left arm was bleeding. He could thwart thirty ripostes, but not the thirty-first, and now his shoulder bled.

The wounds were not yet grave, but they kept on coming as they dodged across the stones, and then the man in black found himself amidst the trees and that was bad for him, so he all but fled before Inigo's onslaught, and then he was in the open again, but Inigo kept coming, nothing could stop him, and then the man in black was back among the boulders, and that was even worse for him than the trees and he shouted out in frustration and practically ran to where there was no open space again.

But there was no dealing with the wizard, and slowly, again, the deadly Cliffs became a factor in the fight, only now it was the man in black who was being forced to doom. He was brave, and he was strong, and the cuts did not make him beg for mercy, and he showed no fear behind his black mask. "You are amazing," he cried, as Inigo increased the already blinding speed of the blade.

"Thank you. It has not come without effort."

The death moment was at hand now. Again and again Inigo thrust forward, and again and again the man in black managed to ward off the attacks, but each time it was harder, and the strength in Inigo's wrists was endless and he only thrust more fiercely and soon the man in black grew weak. "You cannot tell it," he said then "because I wear a cape and mask. But I am smiling now."

"Why?"

"Because I'm not left-handed either," said the man in black. (pp. 128–30)

When he realizes that Inigo has failed to stop the man in black, Vizzini orders Fezzik to eliminate the would-be rescuer. Unlike Inigo, whose failures led him to crime, Fezzik's success as the greatest fighter in the world spoiled him. So strong that no ten men could compete against him, Fezzik lost his job as premier fighter in a circus and turned to Vizzini, who needed his skills. Engaging the man in black on a narrow mountain trail,

Fezzik lifted.
And squeezed.
And squeezed.
Then he took the remains of the man in black, snapped him one way, snapped him the other, cracked him with one hand in the neck, with the other at the spine base, locked his legs up, rolled his limp arms around them, and tossed the entire bundle of what had once been human into a nearby crevice.
That was the theory, anyway.
In fact, what happened was this:
Fezzik lifted.
And squeezed.
And the man in black slipped free. (p. 146)

Goldman's delightful technique of leading the reader to believe one thing when another has occurred sets the reader up for a series of later reversals in which Morgenstern's descriptions are actually fulfilled.

Leaving Fezzik, as he left Inigo, unconscious, the man in black moves on to the top of the mountain where he outwits and murders the conceited Vizzini. Returning with Buttercup to the Cliffs of Insanity, the man in black is prevented from escaping with his prize by Prince Humperdinck's armada, which has cut him off from his ship. While the man in black surveys his enemy's position, Buttercup pushes her latest abductor over the cliff. Before escaping to her prince, however, she surveys what she has done and discovers that the man in black is her lost love, Westley.

Later revived and reunited with Buttercup, Westley finds himself cornered in a fire swamp by Prince Humperdinck, who agrees to spare the young hero's life if Buttercup will return to Florin and become its queen. To save her lover's life and avoid risking the hazards of escape, Buttercup agrees to the prince's proposal, which contains the unstated clause that Westley will spend the rest of his days in a torture chamber.

Regaining consciousness on the mountain, Fezzik joins Prince Humperdinck's Brute Squad, where he notices Count Rugen's six-fingered hand. After being reunited with Inigo during a purge of the Thieves' Quarter, Fezzik describes the count to his friend, who decides to enlist the brains of the man in black in order to revenge his own father's death. Buttercup, meanwhile, is hoping that Westley will return to Florin and save her from marrying Prince Humperdinck.

Providing the reader with a thematic perspective for what is to follow, the fictionalized Goldman interrupts Morgenstern's narrative:

All those Columbia experts can spiel all they want about the delicious satire; they're crazy. This book says 'life isn't fair' and I'm telling you, one and all, you better believe it. . . . I'm not about to tell you this book has a tragic ending, I already said in the very first line how it was my favorite book . . . but there's a lot of bad stuff coming up, torture you've already been prepared for, but there's worse. There's death coming up, and you better understand this: *some of the wrong people die.* . . . Nobody warned me and it was my mistake, so I'm not letting it happen to you. The wrong people die, some of them, and the reason is this: life is not fair. (pp. 205–6)

Inigo and Fezzik make their way into the prince's castle, but they are too late to save Westley, who has been tortured by Count Rugen and finally murdered by Humperdinck. Distraught, they bring Westley to Max, Humperdinck's fired Miracle Man, who, excited by the prospect of avenging his dismissal, brings the fallen hero back to life. The newly formed trio of Westley, Inigo, and Fezzik successfully reenter the castle, but do not arrive in time to prevent Humperdinck from marrying Buttercup. Nevertheless, Westley reaches the princess' bedchamber before she can commit suicide. While Westley saves Buttercup, Fezzik breaks down doors, cracks skulls, and finds four horses with which to escape; Inigo revenges the death of his beloved father when Count Rugen dies of fright at the thought of having his heart cut out. Reunited, the four are prevented from escaping by the Brute Squad until Buttercup asserts her authority as queen and orders Humperdinck's men to run and save their prince. The protagonists flee into the countryside, and are supposed to live happily ever after, but Inigo's wound reopens, Westley has a relapse, Fezzik takes a wrong turn, Buttercup's horse throws a shoe, and "the night behind them was filled with the crescendoing sound of pursuit . . ." (p. 308).

Discarding realism completely in *The Princess Bride*, Goldman presents an elaborately structured plot, a score of incredible coincidences, a host of caricatures, a few irrelevant digressions, and a purposely exaggerated narrative style. Although these combinations represent a new direction for Goldman, they do not indicate an intention to join the "Novel-is-Dead" theorists, who believe that the novel can no longer function in its traditional manner and still continue as a viable art form, that the new novel should exist solely as an art form, never as a testament. Rather than join this antinovel bandwagon, Goldman returns to the point where the novel began in order to create a work that tries not directly to represent life but to present a representation of a representation of life. Such imitation is how novels first came into being with *Don Quixote* imitating *Amadis of Gaul* or Henry Fielding parodying Samuel Richardson's *Pamela*. Reintroducing to literature the prototypic characters and the narrative form of romantic adventure, Goldman's updated "abridgement" is much more serious than its playful artificial aspects indicate.

Goldman chooses to keep the novel alive by creating a new way of employing traditional narrative techniques. In presenting his comment on our chaotic and meaningless universe, Goldman uses conventional novelistic methods. Without following the example of European novelists like Beckett and Robbe-Grillet, who abandoned the traditional novel for more experimental forms, nor blindly accepting the declarations of Susan Sontag, Norman Mailer, Norman Podoretz, and Leslie Fiedler, who have classified conventional novel devices as obsolete, Goldman manages to depart from the traditional novel without adopting an antinovelist style as an alternative. Instead, he continues to employ conventional novel devices, but he uses them ironically, even farcically. Hence, Goldman can mock the traditional novel as obsolete while simultaneously employing its conventions in vitally new ways. The result, *The Princess Bride*, represents a significant innovation in the development of the American novel.

As an artifice of life's illusions, *The Princess Bride* is a paradigm of the fantasies encountered in *No Way to Treat a Lady* and *Father's Day*. Having abandoned the objective reality of these novels, Goldman uses the artifice of *The Princess Bride* to expose the artificiality of his earlier protagonists' illusions. By presenting in the guise of romantic adventure a picture of the world as it is erroneously conceived to be, Goldman has succeeded in creating a fable that, true to fable form, is surrealistic. Paradoxically. Goldman's seemingly lightweight fairy tale is his most serious and most affecting book to date.

Although softened by the adventurous passages, Goldman's exposure of romantic illusion in *The Princess Bride* involves considerable pain. Nowhere in the novel is the pain of unfulfilled romantic expectation better expressed than when the fictitious Goldman tells his son:

'Billy, you got pneumonia; you're taking this book very serious, I know, because we already fought once about it.'

'I'm not fighting any more—'

'Listen to me—I never lied to you yet, did I? Okay. Trust me. I don't want to read you the rest of this chapter, and I want you to say it's all right.'

'Why? What happens in the rest of the chapter?'

'If I *tell* you, I could accomplish the same by reading. Just say okay.'

'I can't say that until I know what happens.'

'But—'

'Tell me what happens and I'll tell you if it's okay and I promise if I don't want to hear it, you can skip to Inigo.'

'You won't do me the favor?'

'I'll sneak out of bed when you're asleep; I don't care where you hide the book, I'll find it and I'll read the rest of the chapter myself, so you might as well tell me.'

'Billy, please?'

'I gotcha; you might as well admit it.'

My father sighed this terrible sound.

I knew I had him beaten then.

'Westley dies,' my father said.

'I said, "What do you mean, 'Westley dies.' " You mean *dies*.

My father nodded. 'Prince Humperdinck kills him.'

'He's only faking though, right?' My father shook his head, closed the book all the way. 'Aw shit,' I said and I started to cry.

'I'm sorry,' my father said, 'I'll leave you alone,' and he left me.

'Who gets Humperdinck?' I screamed at him.

He stopped in the hall. 'I don't understand.'

'Who kills *Prince Humperdinck?* At the end, somebody's got to get him. Is it Fezzik? Who?'

'Nobody kills him. He lives.'

'You mean he wins, Daddy? Jesus, what did you read me this for?' and I buried my head in my pillow and I never cried like that again, not once to this day. I could almost feel my heart emptying into my pillow. (pp. 242–43)

I cite this passage at length not only because Billy's discovery that life is not what it should be reduces him to tears but also because Goldman has remarked that the scene also brought him to tears while he was writing it.

Disappointment in life's expectations is only one of the many levels of pain presented in *The Princess Bride.* Fezzik's mother tells her son, "Life is pain. . . . Anybody that says different is selling something" (p. 140). When the man in black rescues Buttercup, he tests her love for the lost Westley by asking her, "Were you sorry? Did you feel pain? Admit that you felt nothing—" To which the distraught Buttercup responds, "Do not mock my grief! *I died that day*" (p. 159). After capturing Buttercup and Westley, Prince Humperdinck tells Count Rugen, "I said *I* would not hurt him. But I never for a moment said he would not suffer pain. *You* will do the actual tormenting; I will only spectate" (p. 186).

While torturing Westley, Count Rugen keeps an observation report from which he hopes to write the definitive study on mental and physical distress. Before placing Westley on the Machine, he tells him: "One of my theories . . . is that pain involves anticipation. Nothing original, I admit, but I'm going to demonstrate to you what I mean. I will not, underline *not*, use the Machine on you this evening. I could . . . . But instead I will simply erect it and leave it beside you, for you to stare at for the next twenty-four hours, wondering just what it is and how it works and can it really be as dreadful as all that" (p. 223). When the Machine is applied to Westley, his screams can be heard throughout Florin: "Inigo grabbed the giant and the words began pouring out: 'Fezzik—Fezzik—that is the sound of Ultimate Suffering—I know that sound—that was the sound in my heart when Count Rugen slaughtered my father and I saw him fall—the man in black makes it now—' " (p. 245). Finally, when Westley and Buttercup are reunited in her bedchamber, they are interrupted by Prince Humperdinck, who advances on Westley with the words, "To the death." Westley responds by softly shaking his head. "No," he corrects, "To the pain" (p. 298). Goldman's continued use of pain-ridden incidents that can neither be prepared for nor avoided underscores his central theme that "we're not created equal, . . . life isn't fair. I got a cold wife; she's brilliant, she's stimulating, she's terrific; there's no love; that's okay too, just so long as we don't keep expecting everything to somehow even out for us before we die" (p. 205).

In its treatment of pain and disappointment, *The Princess Bride* expresses much of what is implicit in all of Goldman's previous novels, but it also provides a way to affirm the importance of living without avoiding the bleak aspects of contemporary reality. Whereas the protagonists of Goldman's earlier novels affirmed their pathetic lives in negative ways such as geographical escape, daydreams, life-negating fantasies, and suicides, the heroes of *The Princess Bride* affirm their lives through a love and devotion that emphasize life's specialness.

As several good novelists have done before him, Goldman began writing a children's book, but completed an allegory designed to make its readers revalue the ordinary in life and consequently rediscover the beauty hidden within it. Unlike traditional allegories, however, the basic meanings embodied in each of Goldman's heroes suggest a perspective of life rather than an absolute truth. Symbols of rebirth and renewal, Westley, Buttercup, Inigo, and Fezzik represent a positive energy, the absence of which reduces society to a wasteland. Opposing them are Prince Humperdinck and Count Rugen, who annihilating powers seek to destroy life by controlling it. The terrifying sound of Ultimate Suffering, which is identified by Inigo, who had his inner life torn from him when his father was murdered, has two meanings: it represents the pain experienced when life is taken from someone who knows its value, but it is also humanity's plea to be saved from wasteland makers.

Because the temporal power is on his side, as symbolized by the Machine that literally drains the life from its victims, the greedy and selfish Prince Humperdinck can never be vanquished, but he can be foiled occasionally by heroes who are willing to battle for the love that makes life special. Knowing the impossibility of permanently defeating Prince Humperdinck, Westley, Buttercup, Inigo, and Fezzik cannot live happily ever after, but must constantly renew their victory of compassion and hope.

When combined and considered as a whole, Goldman's characters form an image of what it is like to be human. While his heroes represent the fertile and potent side of humanity, Goldman's loveless villains stand for the spiritual maladies to be cured in everyone. That this cure lies in the ordinary rather than in the sophisticated is evidenced in the humble backgrounds and attitudes of the four heroes, who, while cherishing life's special value, the ability and willingness to love, struggle to affirm their lives against the unbeatable forces that work to control their destiny. "Love is the best thing in the world," says Goldman, "but . . . life isn't fair. It's just fairer than death, that's all" (p. 308).

After finishing *The Princess Bride*, while Goldman says he was still "in fantasy world," he tried his hand at a true children's book, *Wigger*, named for a blanket belonging to his daughter Susanna. For her it is a kind of security symbol. In the story, Susanna is an orphan; and, on her way to a home, a bank robber steals Wigger for a disguise. Susanna begins to cry—internally when the head of the orphan home threatens her. She is taken to a hospital where she is diagnosed as dying from drowning. Meanwhile Wigger escapes with the bank robber, who throws "her" out. She is picked up by a variety of people—the last one an artist who makes a flag out of her. Just as Susanna is about to cross the threshold of death, a gust of wind blows Wigger from Switzerland to the hospital in the United States, and the blanket's return saves the little girl.

Writing children's books has become a highly specialized activity; and newcomers—even established writers of other books—are not likely to be very successful in entering the market. Goldman needed the advice of an editor experienced in such matters. His excursion into this domain made little impression. The publishers can locate no reviews of *Wigger*, and it seems to have been unnoticed except for a two-inch announcement of its publication in *Booklist*. His subsequent writings have had fantastic aspects, but they have distinctly not been aimed at the juvenile trade.

CHAPTER 8

Fabulous Escape

I Marathon Man

M   *arathon Man,* I think is despicable. It's done extraordinarily well, having been sold today [4 February 1976] in its
twelfth country. This has never happened before. So obviously people
around the world, at least from Japan to Brazil, must see something in that book. It's sold over a million copies in paperback, and
is going to be a major motion picture. So there are things saying,
'You're pleasing people,' but all I know is I thought it was terrible.
I was dissatisfied when I wrote it.

"It has one interesting thing. How can I put this to you? Hiram
Hayden was my editor from 1960 until he died in 1974, from
Soldier in the Rain through *The Princess Bride,* and there were
certain books that Hiram could not deal with. Hiram was editor of
The American Scholar, a Ph.D., and an extraordinarily bright professor. You have to understand that most editors are basically
illiterate. They haven't read anything before the year they became
editors. Hiram was the only editor I ever met who was better read
than I was. I don't mean that I'm that well read, but there are
certain books I wouldn't have written if it hadn't have been for
Hiram. My pattern until his death was to write a book and give it
to him, and he would look at it, and I would make very little
money. The books did not sell well in hardcover. When Hiram
died and I left Harcourt, my California agent made a three-book
deal, which I'm now two-thirds of the way through, but the whole
editorial process is different now. I would never have written
Marathon Man, for example, if Hiram had been alive.

"Anyway, what's interesting about *Marathon Man* from a
writer's point of view is: I bring Eichmann to New York for a
logical reason. Whether it was Eichmann or Engle or whoever, I
bring a major Nazi to the biggest Jewish city in the world. Well no

one ever said, 'Why does that German come to this Jewish place?'
because that's very skillful. But the reality is, I don't like the book
and I can't help the fact that it seems to work for certain people"
(WG).

Like *The Princess Bride*, *Marathon Man* (1974) provides
Goldman's readers with the chance to escape from their everyday
reality and embrace the reality of an action-packed adventure.
Although it lacks the immediate social relevance of *The Princess
Bride*, in which the author was "wildly close" to his "subconscious," Goldman's thriller about marathon runners, Columbia
graduate students, New York City street kids, jewel smugglers,
family ties, and expert torturers does reflect his concern with the
Jewish genocide of World War II, the intellectual and moral sur-
roundings of the Joseph McCarthy period, the paranoia of secret
agents, inherited guilt, and the necessity to overcome it. Perhaps
because the narrative techniques of *Marathon Man* overshadow its
deeper significance, Goldman is dissatisfied with his ninth novel.
Nevertheless, *Marathon Man* is Goldman's most skillfully structured narrative.

Eliminating from his style the coincidences, caricatures, and
digressions prevalent in *The Princess Bride*, Goldman's story
moves as quickly and as efficiently as the sword fight scene between Inigo Montoya and the man in black. Because its substantial
issues are obscured by the narrative craft Goldman has brought to
perfection, however, *Marathon Man* did not receive the over-
whelming critical praise that his preceding novel did. Anne Ber-
nays of the *Boston Globe* claimed *Marathon Man* to be "unsatisfying either as 'truth' or entertainment," while Philip Ward Burton,
writing in the *Auburn Citizen News*, points out that Goldman
writes entertainingly "but it is difficult to take his plot and characters seriously." Even some of the good reviews sounded bad. The
Washington Star-News reported that "*Marathon Man* may have
offered stiff competition to such classic enjoyments as sex and
fattening foods." Nevertheless, there were reviews that appreciated Goldman's narrative abilities and the book's thematic
substance. Said the *Washington Post*, "There are two literary virtues that one wishes hadn't become clichés: 'It's a good read' and
'It exists on several levels.' One wishes these hadn't become
clichés because they are the two obvious virtues of William
Goldman's *Marathon Man*. It is one hell of a read. And it does
exist on several levels, all of them *superb*." In his review for the

Los Angeles Times, Robert Kirsch accurately describes two levels of Goldman's narrative and their effects:

> The problem is that there are two novels here—one realistic, credible, psychologically valid, the other wild, surreal, taking its force from sensation and violence. The two novels merge in plot, but there is no organic melding. That the story grips you from beginning to end is a tribute to Goldman's undoubted talents as a writer, but at the end a sense of satisfaction and resolution is absent. The reader is left with the same disappointment which comes when he sees through the illusionist's tricks. . . . What pains me is that it might have been a great novel, the best Goldman has yet produced.

After a preliminary chapter that describes two cantankerous old men, Rosenbaum and Hesse, who engage each other in an impromptu car race that leads to their deaths, Goldman introduces Thomas Babington (Babe) Levy, who, when not daydreaming about beating the legendary long-distance man, Nurmi, while jogging around the Central Park reservoir, works on a Doctor of Philosophy degree in history at Columbia University. The subject of Levy's proposed dissertation includes a chapter on the tyrannical purges of the McCarthy period, during which Levy's father, a noted historian, committed suicide. No longer able to bear the distress brought upon him by antiprogressive forces in McCarthy's camp, H. V. Levy shot himself with a gun that Babe has since learned to handle expertly.

When young Levy falls in love with a beautiful Swiss, Elsa Opel, he invites his older brother, Doc, to come to New York to meet her. After introducing them, Doc, a well-traveled businessman, exposes Elsa as German and accuses her of wanting to marry Babe so that she can live permanently in the United States. Embarrassed by her exposure and not knowing how to respond to Doc's accusation, Elsa flees the restaurant in which they have met. Unsuccessful in his attempts to follow her, Babe returns to his apartment where he is soon joined by his brother, who has been mortally wounded.

Interspersed among the eleven chapters that bring the reader to this point in Babe's story are five others that relate the adventures of Scylla, who is named after not the female monster but the rock to which she was fastened. A jewel smuggler who has been caught stealing from the top, Scylla kills several of the agents hired to "retire" him before being stabbed by his employer, a German expatriate whose permanent residence since World War II has been Paraguay. Fulfilling a deep desire to die with someone who loves him, the mortally wounded Scylla drags himself to Babe's apartment and dies in his brother's arms fifty seconds after his arrival.

Shortly after the police, whom he has called, leave his apartment, Babe is kidnapped by Karl and Erhard, who deliver him to Scylla's employer. Once the head of a Nazi concentration camp, Christian Szell has been forced to leave has retreat in Paraguay to retrieve the jewels kept in the safe deposit box of his father, who was accidentally killed while racing another car along the streets of Manhattan. Believing Scylla to have been planning a heist of the jewels taken as bribes from betrayed Jews, Szell, a dentist, expertly tortures Babe by drilling through the nerves in his teeth in order to extract whatever information his brother may have revealed before his death. When Szell momentarily steps outside of the room, Janeway, the police officer in charge of the murder investigation, dramatically kills Karl and Erhard and rescues the greatly relieved Babe.

Having been informed of Szell's background, Babe is shocked by the discovery of his brother's professional associations, which Doc had kept secret from him, but he is still unable to relate information that he has never received. Consequently, Janeway, who was once Doc-Scylla's homosexual lover, reveals his true colors by returning Babe to Szell and his two assistants, who are very much alive.

Eventually convinced that Babe knows nothing about a robbery, Szell orders Janeway, Karl, and Erhard to kill the aspiring marathon man. In a moment when his murderers' guard is relaxed, however, Babe eludes their grasp and uses all his physical and imaginative powers to escape them. With the help of fantasies about Nurmi and other running greats, his dissertation advisor, and his neighborhood's leading juvenile delinquents, Babe retrieves his Adias sneakers and his father's gun from the apartment in which Szell's three cronies are waiting for him. Meeting Babe with a hastily borrowed car, Elsa drives her lover to a deserted cabin where Babe reveals his knowledge of Elsa's part in the plot to "retire" him. When Janeway, Karl, and Erhard arrive, Babe kills them and threatens Elsa with her life if she does not reveal the name of the bank containing the jewels. While Babe makes his way to the bank on Ninety-first Street and Madison Avenue, Szell scouts the midtown diamond exchanges for prices on his ill-gotten jewels. Not knowing about the high concentration of Jews in this area, Szell is soon recognized as "der Weisser Engel." Using the knife that killed Scylla, Szell frees himself from one of his pursuers, grabs a vacant taxi, arrives at his father's bank, and recovers the jewels from the safe deposit box. He is prevented from escaping with them, however, by Babe, who executes the Nazi leader and then distributes his jewels throughout the bottom of the Central Park reservoir before being arrested by a rookie police officer.

Like *The Princess Bride*, *Marathon Man* differs from Goldman's first seven novels in that it does not deal directly with either social manners or the failure of social values. Characterized by an ornate style, *Marathon Man* presents characters and events that seem to have little substance beyond the narrative decoration Goldman gives them. With the exception of Babe, who is both a closet jock and a would-be scholar, and Doc, who is both a murderer and a loving brother, all the other characters in the book are one-dimensional and border on being allegorical. However, unlike *The Princess Bride*, which uses its artificial style to expose the illusions of romantic expectation, *Marathon Man's* artifice, which is enhanced by several cinematographic effects, attempts to give a small measure of significance to the evil and guilt prevalent in a valueless society.

Representing evil are the Joseph McCarthy bureaucrats, who paranoically persecute innocent progressives, and Christian Szell, who kills Scylla and tortures Babe with the same methods he used as head of the Jewish experimental center at Auschwitz. Like the authority figures of *The Princess Bride*, McCarthy and Szell are wasteland makers who try to control other people's destinies. Lacking humanitarian values, McCarthy's purge of the intellectual community in America caused Babe's father to be blackballed from academic institutions and led to his eventual suicide. As much of an authority on pain as Count Rugen of *The Princess Bride*, Szell tortures Babe with a dentist's drill to discover whether Scylla had planned to rob the Nazi experimenter. Later, when Babe prepares his revenge, he uses the pain in his drilled tooth to dehumanize himself: " . . . 'just inhale, *inhale*,' and he pulled the air sharply, forcing it against the open nerves, tight gasping the only sound in the room. Babe kept right on inhaling and oh, but it hurt, Christ it was terrible, but it was necessary. If he was ever going to do what he had to do, he needed all the pain he could get" (p. 274).[1]

That the reaction of a Columbia University graduate student, whose only interest beyond historical research is jogging, should be so violent is not surprising. Violence is practically a Levy family trait. To atone for the pain he has caused to be inflicted upon his family, Professor Levy shoots himself; to remove the guilt of his inaction at the time of his father's death, Doc becomes a dangerous man in a violent profession. To absolve himself from the same guilt that his older brother feels and to avoid a similar guilt in regard to Doc's death, Babe, like Morris Brummell of *No Way to Treat a Lady*, takes the law into his own hands and becomes a murderer as well as a revenger.

In spite of Goldman's attempt to make a universal statement regarding the Jewish genocide, tyrannical democracies, and the unjustified suffering of innocent men and women, *Marathon Man*, at its core, lacks significant reference to the social world because the meaning of Babe's problems exists mostly within the context of his own story. Similarly, every other character in the novel seems to be Goldman's private projection of a contextual good or evil. What little insight into human nature the book offers is on the relatively common level of physical pain, however extraordinary, and guilt. Szell, Janeway, Karl, and Erhard may provoke feelings of horror in the reader, or, in terms of their grotesque ingenuities, may even be considered amusing, but unlike Goldman's previous characters, their meaning is basically indefinable outside of the novel. Furthermore, whereas the themes of *The Princess Bride* and those of Goldman's previous fabulous novel, *No Way to Treat a Lady*, extend beyond their narrative borders, those of *Marathon Man*, for the most part, do not.

Enhancing the novel's prose is the cinematographic structure into which Goldman places his story. Although less than three hundred pages long, *Marathon Man* is divided into thirty chapters. So short are these chapters, and so different from one another in terms of their setting and action, they flash by the reader like scenes in a movie. Becasue of their length, Goldman can keep simultaneously occurring stories running vividly in the reader's imagination for half the book without making any connections between them. When the individual stories eventually come together, Goldman continues flashing different scenes containing markedly different actions at such a pace that the reader visually sprints to the novel's conclusion. Reading *Marathon Man*, then, becomes as close to a cinematic and athletic experience as literature can provide.

As technically perfect and fascinating as Goldman's novel may be, its contextually limited meaning does not mark a significant achievement for a man of his talent. When read in light of such humanly perceptive works as *The Princess Bride* and *Father's Day*, Goldman's disappointment in a book that replaces significant insight into human nature with a detached treatment of a few of life's universal issues is understandable. As pure entertainment, *Marathon Man* may be one of the best novels ever written, but its emphasis on surface action and strongly drawn but only partially substantial characters keep it from being a great novel.

II Magic

"I have a new novel called *Magic,* and in it there is a long eight-page scene in which a father, who is a sports freak, tells his son, who hates sports and whom the father has been trying to make into a football player, about something that he saw when he was very young. The father explains how a football player named Bronko Nagurski came back and won a championship game for the Chicago Bears under incredible circumstances. It was basically the high point of my life too. It was the only time, I suppose, anybody ever came through under pressure.

"My editor on this book, who is a woman—now that Hayden is dead, I've had two editors on my last two books—has no interest in sports, nor should she, but she said, 'Cut this scene.' Now, I'm from Chicago, and I saw this when I was twelve, and I said, 'I can't cut it. I have no objection to cutting it'—shading it really, not cutting it out completely—'but basically I don't know how, because it's one of the things in my life that genuinely moves me.'

"Nagurski was a great runner, who retired in 1936 after having been All-American at two positions, and the only man ever to be All-American at two positions, in 1929, and in those days careers were shorter. At forty-three, during the war, he came back to play in the line, not to run with the ball. Then, in the last game of the season, which was if they won it, they got into the championship, and if not, they didn't, the Bears played their crosstown rivals, who were the Cardinals, who have now moved to St. Louis. At any rate, all the Chicago fullbacks got hurt. So, in the third quarter, with the team behind by ten points, Nagurski was put in at fullback, and I had heard about him all my life, and he won the game for them. He came through. It was unbelievable. He gained a hundred yards in one quarter, and then retired back to Minnesota. But the point of all this is that it was so moving to me that I kept saying to my editor, 'I can't cut it down.' I don't know how to because it's one of the few undisguised autobiographical things I've ever written. She said, 'It doesn't advance the plot. It doesn't help the story.' I said, 'I agree.' She was absolutely right. I was totally willing to shave it down, but I found the material so touching, because it had happened to me, that I couldn't" (WG).

As in *Marathon Man*, the reader must make his way well into *Magic* (1976) before its cinematic scenes begin to come together. The complexity of the individual scenes is first indicated by the structure into which they are placed. The novel opens with a one-page first-person quotation by Merlin, Jr., on the importance of illusion in magic; this statement is followed by a third-person flashforward of a hunter who hears screams coming from a cabin. Interspersed with the first eight chapters, which introduce Goldman's protagonist, Corky Withers, a successful magician, and his agent, Ben Greene, from a third-person point of view, are three first-person diary entries that express concern over Corky's recent erratic behavior. The contents of each diary entry are labeled "POLICE EXHIBIT D."

The novel's second section, which substitutes the names of characters in the book for chapter numbers, begins with a flashback to ten-year-old Corky, who is good at whittling, but whose father wants him to play football and attain the glory denied his older brother, who died in an automobile accident. Breaking a leg in his first high school practice, Corky turns to magic, the medium through which he meets and tries to impress Peggy Ann Snow, the school's most attractive cheerleader and the girl of his dreams. Because Corky is intelligent, it is only natural that Peggy should find Ronnie (Duke) Wayne, a local football hero, to be more attractive.

When his father is fired from his job as a Grossinger's masseur, Corky relocates with him to Chicago and then to San Diego, where the old man finally dies. With three thousand dollars in his pocket, Corkey apprentices himself to Merlin, Jr., a Los Angeles Master, who inspires his protegé with his own attitude toward magic and with stories like the one about Goldman's hero, Hobie Baker, recounted in chapter 3: ". . . and Merlin told of Baker, the Princeton kid who was the greatest hockey player of them all and how he used to flash across the rink in total darkness, guiding the puck blind, because if you had to look for it, if you didn't feel without seeing, forget it" (p. 78).[2]

When Merlin, Jr., dies, his adept assistant takes over the magic act, but fails to entertain his first audience successfully. On the brink of asphyxiating himself, and thereby atoning not only for his failure as a magician but also for the guilt he feels for not succeeding in his father's eyes, Corky hears a voice from within himself that persuades him to live.

Whittling a dummy called Fats, Corky creates a persona through which he can externalize his inner voice. Together, Corky and Fats develop a routine in which Corky plays straight man to Fats's degrading jokes. With the help of Corky's agent, Ben Greene, the magician and his alter ego dummy become relatively popular and wealthy. Before crossing the television borderline of weekly national exposure, however, Corky and Fats make a trip to the former's boyhood home in the Catskill Mountains. There, Corky reveals his never-ending affection to Peggy Ann Snow, who married Ronnie Wayne shortly after their high school graduation.

While Ronnie is away on a sales trip, Corky performs a card trick that makes Peggy believe that she and her admirer share telepathic wavelengths. Moved by the possibilities of their relationship, Peggy decides to leave her husband for Corky. Before they can run away, however, a concerned Ben Greene arrives and tries to convince Corky to take the medical exam required by the television corporation interested in airing his act. Inspired by Fats's argument that a medical exam would expose their schizophrenic relationship and threaten his and Peggy's future happiness, Corky murders first the knowledgeable Greene and then Peggy's husband, who had discovered the agent's body.

After disposing of the second body, Corky tells Fats that he and Peggy are going away without him. In an attempt to save himself from abandonment, Fats tells Peggy that the telepathic incidents are nothing more than sleight-of-hand card tricks. Enraged by Corky's deception and beginning to realize the nature of his relationship with Fats, Peggy runs to the solitude of her cabin bedroom. She is soon joined there, however, by Corky, who, through Fats's voice, implores her to receive a wooden heart he has whittled as a going-away present. Touched by Fats's explanation that Corky relied on magic because he lacked personal self-confidence, Peggy opens her locked bedroom door and accepts the wooden heart, but she is startled by the knives that Corky is holding in his hands.

Leading the reader to believe that Peggy has been murdered and that Corky is completely controlled by Fats, Goldman returns his magician to his cabin, where Fats tells him:

. . . it's time we did a little serious changing in the act, so let me hit you with a couple notions; what say we cut down on the magic and replace it with me doing a couple snazzy musical numbers, say you like it."
    "I like it."

"Good, I kind of had a feeling you would because . . . because . . ."

"What's wrong?"

"I don't know how to say this since I haven't got a stomach, but my stomach hurts."

"Bad?"

"Getting . . . bad."

. . . " . . . after I gave her the . . . heart . . . on my way back down . . . I put them deep in me . . ." (pp. 240–41)

In the sixteenth chapter of part 3, which covers the time of Corky's return to the Catskills, Peggy decides that "even though she didn't love him, Corky's kind of talent you had to string along with, and with that thought firmly in mind, she went down to the cabin to tell him so . . ." (p. 243). Her ensuing screams are heard by the old hunter, who was introduced on the second page of the novel. Similarly, the title of part 1, "Effect," in which excerpts from Fats's diary are marked as police exhibits, is also clarified.

Through the relationship of Corky and his alter ego, Goldman explores the violent terror of mankind's inner desire for self-destruction. Whereas in *Marathon Man* death was presented as an end imposed on Goldman's protagonist by his brother's associates, death in *Magic* is seen as an unconscious desire. When Corky's unconscious wish to destroy himself joins forces with the conditions of his professional career and longing for Peggy Ann Snow, it sets in motion a pattern of guilts and fears that ends in a series of violent murders. After murdering Ben Greene and Ronnie Wayne, Corky realizes that only his own death can recall the unconscious forces he has set loose to conspire against the external world.

Near the core of man's passion for death, Goldman seems to be saying, is perverted love. Tainted by his fear of failure and the guilt stemming from his reliance on magic to secure Peggy's affection, Corky's love for his childhood sweetheart contributes as much to his death as Fats's ambition.

Corky's inner desires to succeed in love and magic launch him on his pursuit of destruction, but there are external conditions that seem almost to conspire with his desire to do himself in. At the peak of his success with Peggy, Corky is visited by Ben Greene, who wants the magician to return with him to New York and be examined by a doctor. No sooner does Corky dispose of his agent's body than Ronnie Wayne returns from his sales trip, interrupts Corky's pursuit of Peggy's affection, and discovers Ben Greene floating in Lake Melody.

How much control the unconscious has over man's life and how much external forces have seems to be one of the major questions of Goldman's concern. A partial answer lies in Corky's suicide, which seems to indicate that the roots of man's desire for destruction rest within the individual's unconscious mind.

While *Magic* ends with the affirmation of Corky's victory over his unconscious mind's persona, Fats, Goldman seems to insist that schizophrenia, guilt, fear, perversion, and the longing for death that characterize contemporary society begin with the individual's deep need for love. When tarnished by certain external forces, however, love fails as an adequate means of affirmation and, in *Magic*, leads Corky to his unwilling embrace of violence and terror. Nevertheless, Goldman credits violence with being an affirmative action. In *Marathon Man*, Babe revenges his brother's death by killing those responsible; in this novel, Corky releases himself from his alter ego's control and atones for his murders by taking his own life.

Like Count Rugen of *The Princess Bride* and Christian Szell of *Marathon Man*, Fats is an authority on pain and uses it to hasten Corky's end. After motivating Corky to murder, Fats tells Peggy that her telepathic powers are nothing more than a card trick. When asked why he exposed Corky, Fats replies that he did it to cause psychological pain and to protect his place in their relationship.

Goldman's theme, which is startling enough on an individual level, becomes politically intriguing with Fats's mention of Dick Nixon. How many public Corkys are turning loose their unconscious minds and equipping them with the large-scale means to kill and confuse with illusion? One way of moving beyond the Vietnam-Watergate wasteland is through individually redeeming gestures. Goldman is not recommending suicide, of course, but rather the effort necessary to control our unconscious lust for death.

Extreme, violent, and blurred by a schizophrenic blending of fact and fantasy, Goldman's vision reveals his fear that man has grown weary of contemporary life and pursues death. But it also offers a way to affirm life, namely, by controlling life-negating amibiton and acting upon unperverted concepts of love.

Demonstrating the perceptive insight into human nature that *Marathon Man* lacked, *Magic* presents a protagonist whose psychological complexity approaches that of a Bovary or a Raskolnikov. However, because the characters with whom Corky comes into contact are invariably one-dimensional, Goldman must rely on increased dosages of violence and suspense to move his story. Forced at every step of the way to create a surface action that will match Corky's psychological circumstances, Goldman ends *Magic* with a grotesque suicide that outdoes everything that has led up to it.

CHAPTER 9

On Goldman

O NE cannot speak of any novelist without sooner or later discussing the quality of the narratives he has written. Because a novel's value depends on the ability of the writer to communicate in an interesting way his reactions to his time's public beliefs, Goldman, who in most of his novels has been ahead of his time, has had to wait longer than most authors for academic recognition. The fact that Goldman's novels are not organized according to one fictional kind but follow multiple modes—novel of manners, confessional journal, psychological novel, social satire, romantic parody, black humor novel, detective story, spy novel, radical protest novel, soap opera, absurdist novel, and every conceivable kind of escape novel—has not helped. Unable to place Goldman within the context of any single literary tradition and confused by his success as a novelist, playwright, theater critic, screenplay writer, literary critic, and children's book author, Goldman's reviewers seem overwhelmed by the variety of literary genres that fail to match their expectations consistently.

In spite of his reviewers' perplexity and the indifference of academic critics, Goldman's popular success seems to be assured. His first novel, *The Temple of Gold*, is in its nineteenth paperback printing; his second novel, *Your Turn to Curtsy, My Turn to Bow*, is in its fourteenth; and *Boys and Girls Together*, his fourth book, is in its thirtieth printing. His third novel, *Soldier in the Rain*, which has six paperback printings, has been adapted to film, as has his fifth book, *No Way to Treat a Lady*. Goldman has written and sold his own screenplays for *The Princess Bride*, *Marathon Man*, and *Magic*. Goldman's screenplay adaptation of *All the President's Men* won the New York Drama Critics' Award for the Best Picture of 1976, and the film won for its author an Oscar for the Best Screenplay Adaptation from Another Medium. Following the film version of *Marathon Man* (1976), came another adaptation, *A Bridge Too Far* (1977), the most expensive movie ever made by the Western nations. At the time of this writing, *Magic* is being filmed and will be released sometime in late 1978 or early 1979. *Mr. Horn*, Goldman's first original western screenplay since his award-winning *Butch Cassidy and the Sundance Kid*, will appear as a miniseries for television in 1978.

Perhaps because of his popularity, Goldman has been critically snubbed by scholars. Serious writers are supposed to be dedicated to analysis, rationality, respectability, and gentility. Thus, many popular novelists have been either overlooked or ignored. No doubt Goldman enjoys his popularity, but he has never been one to court his readers', critics', or fellow writers' approbation. He comments: "I care very deeply. On my tombstone, I don't want somebody to write 'screenwriter'. Whatever I am, if it's of any interest, it's expressed in my novels, and I'm not about to have that affected. In other words, I keep that part of my life as pure as possible."

The current of escape, an important theme in American history as well as literature, runs deep through each of Goldman's ten novels. Generally, his protagonists are fleeing a society that encroaches on their desire to lead their own lives, but their flights also include an abandonment of innocence and former values for the discovery of adult realities and the rebirth of new identities. Most of Goldman's escapists are either individuals who no longer believe in the illusions by which they were brought up to live, or else they are impulsively reacting to their own conditioning in the hope of finding something better. They run the gamut from Raymond Trevitt, with his initial trust in the institutions of our society in *The Temple of Gold*, to Corky Withers, whose escape in *Magic* is one of desperation rather than hope. Hopeful or not, the escapes of Goldman's characters are more than just escapes. With the exception of the suicides in *Boys and Girls Together*, *Soldier in the Rain*, and *Magic* and the daydreams of Peter Bell and Eustis Clay, none of the escapes treated in Goldman's novels is permanent. Although Raymond Trevitt of *The Temple of Gold*, all but one of the characters in *Boys and Girls Together*, the heroes in *The Princess Bride*, and Babe Levy of *Marathon Man* will return to the societies they have left, they will not be the innocent people who originally fled them. Some of them may have achieved a greater degree of maturity for themselves, but most of them suggest no substantial growth. Consequently, what seems to be of most importance to Goldman is not the ends of his characters' escapes but rather the experiences of the escapes and the needs that brought them about.

The illusions men and women live by, which often make human

existence more miserable than it need be, provide the core from which all of Goldman's protagonists seek to depart. Ironically, what they escape to is more often than not other illusions. Because of the artificial distinctions society attaches to the illusions it propagates about race, religion, and material gain, rarely are the human needs of society's individual members recognized.

In *The Temple of Gold*, Raymond Trevitt suffers a beating for his well-intentioned overfeeding of his father's fish, rejection by his mother for disturbing a faculty wives' party with the news of his dead dog, the loss of his friendship with a black student of whom his father does not approve, sexual rejection at the hands of Annabelle, who prefers the more prestigious Professor Janes, and failure to attain an editorship he deserves and needs to gain some sense of self-respect. When Raymond's reckless reaction to the forces of an uncompromising, inhuman society inadvertently causes the deaths of his closest friends, he tries to escape the society he knows in Athens, but discovers only frustration and intolerance elsewhere.

In *Your Turn to Curtsy, My Turn to Bow*, Chad Kimberly is driven by his ambition-oriented society into believing that he is Christ. As inhuman in his demands on his disciple as society has been on him, Chad's schizophrenia frightens Peter Bell into a life of escapist daydreaming. Ambition is not the only illusion that drives the protagonists of *Boys and Girls Together* to New York; most of them are escaping from the unbearable circumstances of their home lives. Nevertheless, their hopes for self-improvement are dashed by unsuccessful love affairs, parents who will not release control of them, professional failures, embarrassing social exposures, and suicide. In *Soldier in the Rain*, Eustis Clay, a successful product of the military-economic complex, is more concerned with making easy money and gaining material comforts than about the abuse Jerry Meltzer suffers because of his Jewish heritage or the loss of Maxwell Slaughter through suicide.

Like the illusions fostered by racial and religious prejudice and materialistic ambition, the great American illusions about success also cause unhappiness and frustration. In *The Thing of It Is . . .* and *Father's Day*, the talented and financially successful Amos McCracken spends an enormous amount of money trying to save first his marriage and then his relationship with his daughter. In the end, his guilt-ridden personal failures lead him to create fantasies that enable him to fulfill the images he has of himself but that also pose a serious threat to the safety and well-being of others.

Westley and Buttercup of *The Princess Bride* believe that their love can conquer all, but they discover they also need the help of a muscleman and a wizard swordsman just to escape from the forces that work to control their lives in Florin. "Forget all the garbage your parents put out," says Goldman. "This book says 'life isn't fair' and I'm telling you, one and all, you better believe it" (p. 205).

The Princess Bride is the last novel in which Goldman's characters believe they can escape temporarily from society's life-controlling forces. The protagonists of *Marathon Man* and *Magic* have no time to withdraw and ponder their situation. When they attempt to do so, they are quickly pursued by agents of the wasteland makers and must concentrate all their energies on battling both themselves and the powers that strive to control them. Unlike Amos McCracken of *Father's Day* and Kit Gil of *No Way to Treat a Lady*, Babe Levy of *Marathon Man* and Corky Withers of *Magic* cannot retreat to a fabulous land to try and make themselves whole; they already live in a fabulous land, where they are constantly assaulted by its empirical and psychological facts. Forced to encounter a vast confusion of fact and fiction, to deal with pain and death, and to seek power against forces that are difficult to pinpoint and consequently understand, Babe and Corky must stay rooted in a system that attempts to deny their vitality while creating illusions that life is what it should be. What affirmation Goldman's protagonists can achieve in this world seems to be the small but valuable awareness that life is simply better than death.

As a fabulist of thrillers, some of which come close to providing a cinematic experience, Goldman may be considered an accomplished and inventive storyteller, and, in thematic terms, a serious artist. Though his angle of vision has become increasingly more violent and absurd, he has not given way to despair or cynicism, but has managed to deal with his resignation about the human condition without losing his sense of humor or concern for humanity. Whether he will ever be labeled an important novelist depends on how well the books that incorporate this tempered vision survive the test of time. As they are read today, however, Goldman's works provide an unassailable argument against the novel-is-dead critics and effectively contribute to the life span of our literature's most popular and therefore most important genre.

Notes and References

Chapter Two

1. *The Temple of Gold* (New York: Bantam Books, Inc., 1958). Subsequent page references in the text are to this edition.

Chapter Three

1. Although Goldman's account of Hobie Baker is slightly inflated, the Princeton athlete was something of a hero in his own time. Hobie Baker is also the model for the protagonist in Goldman's screenplay, *The Great Waldo Pepper*, which features actor Robert Redford.

2. *Your Turn to Curtsy, My Turn to Bow* (New York: Bantam Books, Inc., 1959). Subsequent page references in the text are to this edition.

3. In his book, *Radical Innocence: Studies in Contemporary American Literature* (Princeton: Princeton University Press, 1961), Ihab Hassan quotes Dr. Bruno Bettelheim's observation of "how the self seeks refuge in schizophrenia when 'reality' becomes unendurable." Dr. Bettelheim, who was once an inmate of a Nazi concentration camp, was "able to preserve his own sanity only by allowing his consciousness to split up into subject and object, and by assigning to the first a genuinely human role which the indignities of the second could not subvert. The significance of this act reaches far beyond pathological behavior; it confronts us with the unspeakable fact of 'pain' in the world. Schizophrenia, insofar as it entails the withdrawal of libido from real objects and its reversion back to the ego, constitutes the ultimate form of recoil."

4. Commenting on schizophrenia, Hassan notes, "The basic and perhaps irreconcilable struggle, however, is not between man and society. Freud . . . suggests that the self is not only opposed to the world but also divided in its own house. Man, in this pessimistic and perhaps ultimately religious view, is as much his own victim as he is the victim of society."

5. In his article for *The Boston Globe* (June 19, 1968, pp. 19–40), entitled "William Goldman, An Overlooked Young Author Considered," Gregory McDonald concludes his comments on *Your Turn to Curtsy, My Turn to Bow* with the statement: "The publishing business being as it is, first and second novels frequently appear in reverse order."

6. F. Scott Fitzgerald, *The Great Gatsby* (New York: Charles Scribner's Sons, Inc., 1925), p. 2.

7. Ibid., p. 182.

8. Goldman's flashforward is a creative extension of the technique that

begins a story with its conclusion, e.g. *Beau Geste* and the film *Lawrence of Arabia*. Although *Your Turn to Curtsy, My Turn to Bow* precedes *Easy Rider* (1967), the latter is the only popular film to incorporate flashforwards in the same way as Goldman's novel. Perhaps the most memorable flashforward in *Easy Rider* occurs when Captain America (Peter Fonda) stares at a picture in a New Orleans brothel and the audience is given a quick shot of his burning motorcycle. Coincidentally, Fonda made his acting debut in a Goldman play, *Blood, Sweat, and Stanley Poole* (1961).

Chapter Four

1. *Soldier in the Rain* (New York: Bantam Books, Inc., 1960). Subsequent page references in the text are to this edition.

Chapter Five

1. *Boys and Girls Together* (New York: Bantam Books, Inc., 1965). Subsequent page references in the text are to this edition.
2. *No Way to Treat a Lady* (New York: Harcourt, Brace & World, Inc., 1968).

Chapter Six

1. *The Thing of It Is . . .* (New York: Harcourt, Brace & World, Inc., tion.
2. *Butch Cassidy and the Sundance Kid* (New York: Bantam Books, Inc., 1969).
3. *Father's Day* (New York: Harcourt, Brace, Jovanovich, Inc., 1971). Subsequent page references in the text are to this edition.

Chapter Seven

1. One of Goldman's few letters, this account of *The Princess Bride* was found in Goldman's publicity file at Harcourt, Brace, Jovanovich, Inc. Communication between Goldman and his editor, Hayden, was usually either in person or via telephone. There was no date on the letter.
2. *The Princess Bride* (New York: Harcourt, Brace, Jovanovich, Inc., 1973). Subsequent page references in the text are to this edition.

Chapter Eight

1. *Marathon Man* (New York: Delacorte Press, Inc., 1974). Subsequent page references in the text are to this edition.
2. *Magic* (New York: Delacorte Press, Inc. 1976). Subsequent page references in the text are to this edition.

Selected Bibliography

PRIMARY SOURCES

1. Novels
Boys and Girls Together. New York: Atheneum Publishers, 1964. Also available in paperback, New York: Bantam Books, Inc., 1965.
Father's Day. New York: Harcourt, Brace, Jovanovich, Inc., 1971.
Magic. New York: Delacorte Press, 1976. Also available in paperback, New York: Dell Publishing Co., 1977.
Marathon Man. New York: Delacorte Press, 1974. Also available in paperback, New York: Dell Publishing Co., 1975.
No Way to Treat a Lady. New York: Harcourt, Brace & World, Inc., 1968. Originally published under the pseudonym Harry Longbaugh, New York: Fawcett Publications, Inc., 1964.
The Princess Bride. New York: Harcourt, Brace, Jovanovich, Inc., 1973. Also available in paperback, New York: Ballantine Press, Inc., 1974.
Soldier in the Rain. New York: Atheneum Publishers, 1960. Also available in paperback, New York: Bantam Books, Inc., 1965.
The Temple of Gold. New York: Alfred A. Knopf, Inc., 1957. Also available in paperback, New York: Bantam Books, Inc., 1958, and New York: Dell Publishing Co., 1976.
The Thing of It Is . . . . New York: Harcourt, Brace & World, Inc., 1967.
Your Turn to Curtsy, My Turn to Bow. New York: Doubleday & Company, Inc., 1958. Also available in paperback, New York: Bantam Books, Inc., 1960.

2. Children's Story
Wigger. New York: Harcourt, Brace, Jovanovich, Inc., 1974.

3. Short Stories
"Something Blue," *Rogue*, April 1958, pp. 13–83.
"Till the Right Girls Come Along," *Transatlantic Review*, 1958, pp. 50–61.

4. Criticism
"The Good-Bye Look" [a review of the Ross MacDonald novel of the same title], *New York Times Book Review*, June 1, 1969, p. 1.
The Season: A Candid Look at Broadway. New York: Harcourt, Brace & World, Inc., 1969. Also available in paperback, New York: Bantam Books, Inc., 1970.

5. Plays:

Blood, Sweat, and Stanley Poole. Coauthored with James Goldman. New
York: Dramatists Play Service, Inc., 1962. [Opening night on Broadway;
October 6, 1961.]

Family Affair. Coauthored with James Goldman and John Kander. Unpublished. [Opening night on Broadway; January 29, 1962.]

6. Screenplays

All the President's Men. Adapted from the Bob Woodward and Carl
Bernstein book of the same title. Released by Warner Brothers, Inc.
1976.

A Bridge Too Far. Adapted from the Cornelius Ryan book of the same title.
Released by United Artists, Inc., 1977.

Butch Cassidy and the Sundance Kid. An original screenplay New York:
Bantam Books, 1969. [Film released by Twentieth-Century Fox, Inc.,
1969]

The Chill. Unproduced screenplay, a sequel to *Harper*, from the novel by
Ross MacDonald, 1967.

The Great Waldo Pepper. An original screenplay. Released by Universal
Pictures, Inc., 1975.

Harper. Adapted from *The Moving Target*, a novel by Ross MacDonald.
Released by Warner Brothers, Inc., 1966.

The Hot Rock. Adapted from the Donald Westlake novel of the same title.
Released by Twentieth-Century Fox, Inc., 1972.

In The Spring The War Ended. Unproduced screenplay adapted from the
Steven Linakis novel of the same title, 1968.

Magic. Adapted from the novel of the same title. Purchased by Joseph E.
Levine Presents, Inc.

Marathon Man. Adapted from the novel of the same title. Released by
Warner Brothers, Inc., 1976.

Mr. Horn. An original screenplay purchased by United Artists, Inc. To be
produced as a four-hour miniseries for television in the fall of 1978 and
then released as a feature film in Europe.

The Princess Bride. Unproduced screenplay from the novel of the same title.
Purchased by Twentieth-Century Fox, Inc., 1974.

The Stepford Wives. Adapted from the Ira Levin novel of the same title.
Released by Columbia Pictures, Inc., 1974.

The Thing of It Is . . . Unproduced screenplay from the novel of the same
title, 1970.

SECONDARY SOURCES

1. Articles and Parts of Books

BAHRENBURG, BRUCE. "Underground Writer Gains Paperback Fame," *New
York Times*, 1966. This article focuses attention on Goldman as an

underground author "popular with a wide reading audience but who
remains ignored by the highbrow critics and whose works are absent
from college textbooks."

BARKHAM, JOHN. "Author, Movie-Writer William Goldman Prefers Novels
Over Hollywood Scripts," *Saturday Review*, March 20, 1971. This
article contains an interview with Goldman in which the author talks
about the differences between writing a novel, which is an individual
effort, and writing a screenplay, which is a group endeavor.

FRENCH, WARREN. "William Goldman is *The Thing of It Is* . . . ." *Season of
Promise: Spring Fiction; 1967.* Columbia: University of Missouri Press,
1968, pp. 26–32. Professor French focuses his attention on Goldman's
versatility and craftsmanship in the critically ignored *Your Turn to
Curtsy, My Turn to Bow* and the then recent novel *The Thing of It Is
. . . .*

HIRSCHBERG, JACK. "On Adapting a Best Selling Book to the Screen." *A
Portrait of "All the President's Men."* New York: Warner Books, Inc.,
1976, pp. 90–93. Hirschberg's article contains an interview with
Goldman in which the author expresses his attitude toward screenwrit-
ing and the problems he encountered during the writing of *All The
President's Men.*

MCDONALD, GREGORY. "An Overlooked Young Author Considered," *Boston Globe*, June 19, 1968, pp. 19–40. This important perspective on
Goldman's earliest novels includes the only known review of *Your Turn
to Curtsy, My Turn to Bow.* McDonald compares Goldman to other
contemporary American writers and refers to him as "a peculiar symbol
of the good individual writer living and working in the age of the
committee."

2. Reviews

Boys and Girls Together

KIRSCH, ROBERT. "Goldman Novel Succeeds as 'Fund of Entertainment,' "
Los Angeles Times, June 24, 1964, IV, p. 4. This accurate comment on
Goldman's themes is important for the healing effect it had on Goldman
after he read Conrad Knickerbocker's review of his novel in the *New
York Times.*

KNICKERBOCKER, CONRAD. "Playing the Game," *New York Times Book
Review*, July 26, 1964, p. 24. This somewhat humorous but sadistically
unfair review of Goldman's fourth novel is more important for its effect
on Goldman than for its content.

ROBERTSON, DON. "You're Invited to a Rip-Rousing Party," *Cleveland
Plain Dealer*, July 26, 1964. Robertson says Goldman's novel is "without
question the most exciting piece of American fiction written in this
decade." Robertson's review draws a parallel between Goldman's
characters and the novel's structure.

Father's Day

LEVIN, MARTIN. *"Father's Day," New York Times Book Review*, January 31, 1971, p. 36. Levin's article stresses Goldman's "offhand expertise" at "weaving together flashbacks and current happenings" to compose his protagonist's personality.

LOTTMAN, EILEEN. "Day Out With Jessica," *Providence Sunday Journal*, February 14, 1971. This review points out Goldman's treatment of schizophrenia and "the way despair can bend a mind to the breaking point."

QUICK, JONATHAN. "Goldman's Latest Work is Sequel," *Los Angeles Times*, April 25, 1971. Comparing Goldman to Saul Bellow, J. P. Donleavy, and Edward Albee, Quick maps Amos McCracken's "uproarious and pathetic" failure to escape from reality through fantasy. *"Father's Day* is strongest at moments when Amos' runaway imagination overtakes the narrative. It often happens imperceptibly, leaving the reader unaware of the shift from the actual to the imaginary."

Magic

ANDERSEN, RICHARD. *"Magic," Pride*, October 20, 1976, p. 10. This article talks about Goldman's concern with man's inability to act on traditional concepts of love and his unconscious desire to self-destruct.

LEHMANN-HAUPT, CHRISTOPHER. *"Magic," New York Times*, November 5, 1976, p. 21. The reviewer calls Goldman's book "gripping," and centers his attention on the author's ability to "unfold his plot so as to keep us suspended between puzzlement and anticipation."

WOLFF, JEFFREY. "William Goldman Pulls *Magic* Out of Elliptical Hat," *Los Angeles Times*, October 3, 1976. Wolff discusses the protagonist's "victimization by illusion" and its significance to the reader.

Marathon Man

KIRSCH, ROBERT. "Novel Flawed by Optical Allusion [sic]," *Los Angeles Times*, October 15, 1974. Kirsch talks about the influence of cinematic techniques on Goldman's book: "visual impact, scenic structure, dialogue, and action."

THOMAS, PHIL. "Goldman on Guilt," Associated Press Release, 1974. "Written so smoothly into the fast-flowing action that it doesn't disturb or slow down the narrative is the recurring theme of guilt. On its simplest level, it is the guilt an individual carries with him through the years, . . . On a more complex level, it is guilt borne by people as a mass, the guilt of genocide."

No Way to Treat a Lady

BOUCHER, ANTHONY. "Criminals at Large," *New York Times*, April 14, 1968. This review is important to Goldman because he believes it is the only positive criticism the *New York Times* has printed on any of his novels.

The Princess Bride
FULLER, EDMUND. "A Gothic Put-On and a Rising Tycoon," *Wall Street Journal*, October 30, 1973. Fuller discusses the novel as a loving parody of Gothic romance and concludes: "yet with all its comedy, there are moments when the thing gets to you straight—splendid episodes, with a growing somberness toward the close that sets one to pondering Mr. Goldman's ultimate intentions."

KIRSCH, ROBERT. "Trip Beyond 'Good Parts,'" *Los Angeles Times*, September 14, 1973. This review praises Goldman's idea of the abridgement but centers most of its attention on "an evocation of the kind of experience common in those more innocent days which gave rise to a belief in heroes, in the struggle between evil and good, in fairy tales, and in love, not as opposed to sex but in some sort of unspoken harmony with it."

WALKER, GERALD. *"The Princess Bride,"* *New York Times Book Review*, December 23, 1973, p. 16. Walker discusses Goldman's "abridgement" as "a kind of comedic extension of Brecht's distancing effect, alienation to provoke not an intellectual response, but an entertained response. And it works."

Soldier in the Rain
MITGANG, HERBERT. *"Soldier in the Rain,"* *New York Times*, July 17, 1960, p. 26. Mitgang reads Goldman's novel as "a city novelist's version of a Tennessee ridge-runner."

The Temple of Gold
DEMPSEY, DAVID. *"The Temple of Gold,"* *New York Times*, November 17, 1957, p. 54.

The Thing of It Is . . .
BARKHAM, JOHN. "Man and Wife Apart," *Saturday Review*, April 8, 1967. Barkham discusses Goldman's skill as a "verbal prestidigitator" that "elongates a short story into a novella by sheer narrative virtuosity."

FRENCH, WARREN. "The Man Who Never Told Anyone About Anything," *Kansas City Star*, April 23, 1967, p. 12G. French points out Goldman's concern with "Americans' inability to cope with success": "Perhaps our greatest national problem today is that training for disaster has rendered us unable to communicate in affluent times. Rarely has this situation been dramatized with the success that it is in Goldman's new novel. He speaks for those unable to speak for themselves."

KIRSCH, ROBERT. "Goldman Novel Brief, Witty," *Los Angeles Times*, May 11, 1967, p. 20. "The novel swings between uproariously funny situations and the sad terror of two people who love each other too much to separate and who equally cannot abide each other when together. Goldman manages to resolve this dilemma in an ending as understated as it is undeniably true."

Index

118